# ASIA BOND MONITOR
## NOVEMBER 2023

ASIAN DEVELOPMENT BANK

# Contents

# Emerging East Asian Local Currency Bond Markets: A Regional Update

# Executive Summary

## Recent Developments in Financial Conditions in Emerging East Asia

During the review period from 1 September to 10 November, financial conditions weakened across emerging East Asia on expectations that the United States (US) Federal Reserve would keep interest rates elevated for an extended period.[1] This prospect drove both US dollar appreciation and capital outflows from emerging markets. To prevent inflationary pressure and safeguard financial stability, some regional central banks recently resumed hiking policy rates, including Bank Indonesia, the Bangko Sentral ng Pilipinas, and the Bank of Thailand. Across emerging East Asian financial markets, widened risk premiums, a retreat in equity markets, and weakened currencies were recorded. Continued high interest rates in both advanced economies and regional markets pushed up bond yields during the review period.

With the Federal Reserve expected to keep interest rates high for a longer period, most regional currencies slightly weakened against the US dollar, posting an average depreciation of 1.0% (simple) and 0.4% (gross-domestic-product-weighted) during the review period. Weak external demand and a moderating growth outlook in the People's Republic of China (PRC), combined with the hawkish monetary stance in the US, drove regional equity markets to fall by 4.9% (simple average) and 4.3% (market-weighted average), and for risk premiums, measured by credit default swaps spreads, to widen by 3.3 basis points (simple average) and 1.4 basis points (gross-domestic-product-weighted average). Capital outflows from the region's equity markets amounted to USD17.1 billion during the review period, while bond markets recorded outflows of USD5.9 billion in September.

The risk outlook for regional financial conditions is generally balanced. On the downside, the Federal Reserve's intention to hold interest rates elevated for a longer period will lead to lasting high borrowing costs in regional markets. This will challenge borrowers with significant leverage and a need for liquidity to refinance debt, including some property companies in the PRC and the Government of the Lao People's Democratic Republic. In addition, higher borrowing costs will exacerbate the fiscal burden for governments using fiscal measures to support economic growth, even in economies with sound fundamentals, which will weaken both their fiscal balance and currency. On the upside, inflation across the region is expected to ease next year and over the medium term despite some transitory pressure from the recent uptick in food and oil prices. The expected easing of inflation, combined with a weak external environment and heightened financial risks from higher interest rates, may allow central banks to consider easing monetary conditions to support economic growth.

## Recent Developments in Local Currency Bond Markets in Emerging East Asia

By the end of September, emerging East Asian local currency (LCY) bonds outstanding reached USD23.5 trillion on modest expansions of 2.5% quarter-on-quarter (q-o-q) and 8.2% year-on-year in the third quarter (Q3) of 2023, compared to 2.0% q-o-q and 7.9% year-on-year in the previous quarter. Growth in government bonds rose to 3.0% q-o-q in Q3 2023 from 2.4% q-o-q in the second quarter (Q2) of 2023, driven by increased issuance. Corporate bond market growth was broadly stable, rising 1.5% q-o-q in Q3 2023 versus 1.4% q-o-q in Q2 2023. Government bonds accounted for 62.4% of total LCY bonds outstanding at the end of September. Aggregate LCY bonds outstanding in member markets of the Association of Southeast Asian Nations (ASEAN) reached USD2.1 trillion at the end of September, equivalent to 9.0% of the emerging East Asian total.

---

[1] Emerging East Asia is defined to include member states of the Association of Southeast Asian Nations (ASEAN) plus the People's Republic of China; Hong Kong, China; and the Republic of Korea.

During Q3 2023, emerging East Asian LCY bond issuance totaled USD2.5 trillion on q-o-q growth of 8.6%, nearly doubling Q2 2023's growth of 4.6% q-o-q. Growth in government bond issuance surged 13.2% q-o-q to USD1.1 trillion, up from only 2.3% q-o-q in Q2 2023, driven largely by economic stimulus measures in the PRC. Corporate bond issuance recorded USD0.9 trillion on moderated growth of 5.0% q-o-q, compared with 12.5% q-o-q in the previous quarter. ASEAN markets' total issuance reached USD0.5 trillion, comprising 19.7% of the region's total issuance in Q3 2023.

The majority of LCY Treasury bonds outstanding in emerging East Asia at the end of September carried medium- to long-term tenors. In terms of bonds outstanding, Treasury bonds with maturities of over 5 years comprised 53.7% of the total, while the corresponding share was 55.6% in terms of Q3 2023 issuance. The relatively high share of medium- to long-term tenors among all outstanding Treasury bonds mitigated the impact of high interest rates on fiscal burdens. Treasury bonds in the region had a size-weighted average tenor of 8.7 years for outstanding bonds and 6.3 years for Q3 2023 issuance. Meanwhile, domestic investors held 89.4% of the region's outstanding Treasury bonds at the end of September, contributing to Treasury bonds' price resilience to portfolio outflows. Banks were the largest bond holders in the region, holding more than half of all outstanding Treasury bonds at the end of September.

ASEAN+3 sustainable bonds outstanding reached USD734.1 billion at the end of September following robust issuance of USD57.3 billion in Q3 2023.[2] ASEAN+3's sustainable bond market grew 5.2% q-o-q in Q3 2023, posting the fastest q-o-q growth and the largest quarterly issuance total among major regional sustainable bond markets globally. ASEAN+3 is the second-largest regional sustainable bond market in the world, accounting for 18.9% of total global sustainable bonds, after the European Union (EU-20), which accounts for 37.1%. ASEAN+3's sustainable bond issuance during Q3 2023 comprised 36.3% of total global sustainable bond issuance.

ASEAN+3's sustainable bond market remained small, accounting for only 2.0% of its general bond market. This is much smaller than the corresponding share of 6.7% in the EU-20 market. ASEAN+3 sustainable bond issuance is dominated by LCY financing, with 69.5% of Q3 2023 issuance in domestic currencies. However, this also was below the EU-20's LCY issuance share of 85.8% in Q3 2023. ASEAN+3 sustainable bond issuance in Q3 2023 was concentrated in shorter tenors, with 68.1% of issuances carrying maturities of 5 years or less, compared to the corresponding share of 34.9% in the EU-20. Following Singapore's 50-year SGD2.8 billion green bond issuance in August, ASEAN+3's size-weighted average issuance tenor rose to 7.2 years in Q3 2023, from 4.8 years in Q2 2023, which was roughly on par with 7.6 years in the EU-20.

---

[2] ASEAN+3 is defined to include member states of the Association of Southeast Asian Nations (ASEAN) plus the People's Republic of China; Hong Kong, China; Japan; and the Republic of Korea.

# Developments in Regional Financial Conditions

Financial conditions in emerging East Asian markets weakened from 1 September to 10 November, largely driven by investor expectations that the United States (US) Federal Reserve would keep interest rates higher for longer than earlier anticipated.[1] Inflation in some regional markets also picked up amid elevated food and oil prices during the review period. As a result, emerging East Asian economies experienced a retreat in equity markets, widened risk premiums, currency depreciations against the US dollar, as well as net foreign portfolio outflows. Regional bond yields rose in nearly all markets during the review period, mirroring the upward movement of yields in major advanced economies (**Table A**). Risks to regional financial conditions remained balanced. The downside risk of an extended period of high interest rates posing a threat to financial stability could be offset by factors that support an ending of tight monetary stances, including the expected easing of inflation, headwinds to the economic outlook, and heightened financial risks due to high interest rates.

The rise in long-term bond yields in major advanced economies, especially the US, outpaced the increase in short-term bond yields during the review period, steepening yield curves. Increases in short-term government bond yields in the US and euro area were driven by their respective central banks' decision to hold interest rates higher for longer to address persistent elevated inflation. The rapid rise in long-term bond yields, especially in the US, reflected an increased bond supply and a heavy fiscal burden of rising debt levels and higher interest rates. This was noted by Fitch Ratings when it downgraded the sovereign credit rating of the US from AAA to AA+ on 1 August. In its decision, Fitch Ratings cited an "expected fiscal deterioration in the next [3] years" as well as a high and still growing debt burden as factors for the downgrade. Moody's also revised its US credit rating outlook from stable to negative in November, citing a wider budget deficit. At the end of July, the US Treasury raised its borrowing target in the third quarter to USD1 trillion, which was USD274 billion

**Table A: Changes in Financial Conditions in Major Advanced Economies and Select Emerging East Asian Markets from 1 September 2023 to 10 November 2023**

| | 2-Year Government Bond Yield (bps) | 10-Year Government Bond Yield (bps) | 5-Year Credit Default Swap Spread (bps) | Equity Index (%) | FX Rate (%) |
|---|---|---|---|---|---|
| **Major Advanced Economies** | | | | | |
| Euro Area | 8 | 17 | – | (2.0) | (0.9) |
| Japan | 9 | 22 | 10 | (0.1) | (3.5) |
| United States | 18 | 47 | – | (2.2) | – |
| **Select Emerging East Asian Markets** | | | | | |
| China, People's Rep. of | 22 | 2 | 0.7 | (3.0) | (0.3) |
| Hong Kong, China | 37 | 25 | – | (6.4) | 0.5 |
| Indonesia | 51 | 45 | 5 | (2.4) | (2.9) |
| Korea, Rep. of | 17 | 18 | 4 | (6.0) | 0.1 |
| Malaysia | 4 | 5 | 2 | (1.2) | (1.3) |
| Philippines | 30 | 35 | 3 | (0.3) | 1.1 |
| Singapore | (4) | (4) | – | (3.9) | (0.6) |
| Thailand | 25 | 30 | 3 | (11.0) | (2.5) |
| Viet Nam | 6 | 5 | 5 | (10.0) | (1.0) |

( ) = negative, – = not available, bps = basis points, FX = foreign exchange.

Note: A positive (negative) value for the FX rate indicates the appreciation (depreciation) of the local currency against the United States dollar.

Source: *AsianBondsOnline* calculations based on Bloomberg LP data.

---

[1] Emerging East Asia is defined to include member states of the Association of Southeast Asian Nations (ASEAN) plus the People's Republic of China; Hong Kong, China; and the Republic of Korea.

higher than its initial estimate in May, due to a forecast of lower receipts and higher outlays.[2] The increased supply of US Treasuries needed to finance the deficit pushed up long-term bond yields.

Persistent inflation and a solid job market lent support to the Federal Reserve to maintain higher interest rates for an extended period. The Federal Reserve left the federal funds target rate unchanged at its 19–20 September and 1–2 November Federal Open Market Committee (FOMC) meetings. In its September FOMC meeting, the Federal Reserve raised interest rate forecasts for 2024 and 2025 to 5.1% and 3.9%, respectively, from projections in June of 4.6% and 3.4%. This suggests that the Federal Reserve will keep higher interest rates for longer than previously expected. Subsequently, in its November FOMC statement, the Federal Reserve noted that inflation remains elevated and the labor market has slowed but is still strong. The US inflation rate fell to 3.2% year-on-year (y-o-y) in October over falling energy prices from 3.7% y-o-y in both September and August, but was still above the 2.0% inflation target. Brent crude oil prices had risen to USD95.4 per barrel on 19 September, the highest so far this year, due to supply concerns before falling to USD86.2 per barrel on 5 October as fears of reduced demand from a slowing global economy took hold. The price bounced back to USD94.1 per barrel on 20 October amid the current conflict in the Middle East but had since declined to USD82.6 per barrel by 10 November (**Figure A**). Excluding food and energy, however, core inflation in

the US continued to decline, falling to 4.0% y-o-y in October from 4.1% y-o-y in September and 4.3% y-o-y in August. Nonfarm payrolls declined to 150,000 in October from 297,000 in September. The recent economic performance remained sound in the US, with the annualized quarter-on-quarter gross domestic product (GDP) growth rate climbing to 4.9% in the third quarter (Q3) from 2.1% in the second quarter (Q2) of 2023.

The recent rise in Treasury bond yields, especially long-term bond yields, may suggest there will be no further rate hikes this year. The Federal Reserve noted in its November FOMC meeting that financial conditions have tightened for households and businesses. During the FOMC press conference, Federal Reserve Chair Jerome Powell mentioned that the Federal Reserve will be assessing if there is a need for further rate hikes, fueling speculation that the Federal Reserve is done hiking rates. The CME FedWatch Tool reflected this expectation, with its probability of no rate hike at the December FOMC meeting increasing from 68.9% as of 31 October to 95.2% on 3 November and its probability of 25 basis points (bps) rate hike declining from 28.8% to 4.8% during the same period. Nevertheless, uncertainty remained as Federal Reserve Chair Jerome Powell noted that the FOMC is committed to bring inflation down to its target rate during the International Monetary Fund annual research conference on 9 November. Federal Reserve Governor Christopher Waller on 7 November indicated that the recent US GDP figure was a "blowout" and needs observing. Federal Reserve Governor Michelle Bowman, on 7 November in a speech to the Ohio Bankers League, said that the recent US GDP performance suggests the need for a higher federal funds rate. Dallas Federal Reserve President Lorrie Logan also said that US economic performance has been strong and noted that inflation is still elevated. As a result, the probability of a rate hike at the December FOMC meeting rose to 9.1% as of 10 November.

In the euro area, a weakening economic performance and declining inflation increased the possibility of a halt in rate hikes. The euro area also experienced a rise in both long- and short-term bond yields during the review period as the European Central Bank (ECB) persisted in tightening its monetary policy. The ECB raised its three main interest rates by 25 bps each on 14 September and hinted that current interest rates were now sufficient to

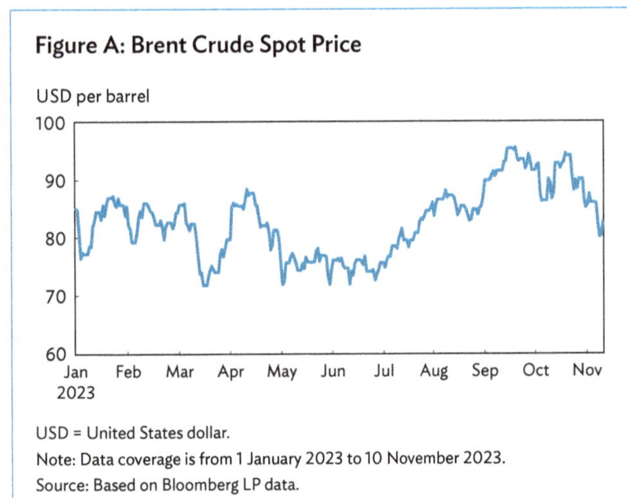

**Figure A: Brent Crude Spot Price**



USD = United States dollar.
Note: Data coverage is from 1 January 2023 to 10 November 2023.
Source: Based on Bloomberg LP data.

---

[2]  US Department of the Treasury. 2023. "Treasury Announces Marketable Borrowing Estimates." Press Release. 31 July.

bring down inflation in the medium-term, suggesting that it will halt its rate hikes. Subsequently, on 26 October, the ECB left policy rates unchanged at their current levels. The ECB observed weakened demand and restrictive financial conditions that could contribute to easing inflationary pressures. Inflation in the euro area eased from 5.2% y-o-y in August to 4.3% y-o-y in September and further to 2.9% y-o-y in October. Recent data confirmed the weakening economic performance in the euro area. GDP growth fell to 0.1% y-o-y in Q3 2023 from 0.5% y-o-y in Q2 2023 and 1.1% y-o-y in the first quarter of 2023. The ECB revised downward its GDP growth forecasts to 0.7% in 2023 and 1.0% for 2024 in September from forecasts of 0.9% and 1.5%, respectively, in June. Meanwhile, amid rising energy prices, the ECB revised upward its inflation projections to 5.6% for 2023 and 3.2% for 2024 in September from June projections of 5.4% and 3.0%, respectively.

During its 31 October monetary policy meeting, the Bank of Japan (BOJ) announced that its previous 1.0% ceiling on the 10-year government bond yield would now be treated more as a reference or guide, and it ceased purchases of 10-year Japan Government Bonds at a fixed yield of 1.0%. The **Box** presents a brief overview of the BOJ's unconventional monetary policy easing measures in the past decade and discusses their impact on the development of domestic bond markets and exchange rates. The BOJ also released updated forecasts in October from its previous ones in June. GDP forecasts were revised to an annualized 2.0% for 2023 and 1.0% for 2024 in October from 1.3% and 1.2%, respectively, in June. Meanwhile, inflation forecasts were adjusted to 2.8% y-o-y in 2023 and 2024, and 1.7% y-o-y in 2025, from June projections of 2.5% y-o-y, 1.9% y-o-y, and 1.6% y-o-y, respectively. In Q3 2023, Japan's GDP shrank an annualized 2.1% after a robust annual growth of 4.5% in Q2 2023. Inflation has been relatively stable in recent months but remained above the BOJ's 2.0% target, with inflation for August at 3.2% y-o-y, September at 3.0% y-o-y, and October at 3.3% y-o-y.

The recent uptick in food and oil prices and expectations of higher interest rate for a longer period in advanced economies increased the possibility of continued tight monetary stances among regional central banks to address inflationary pressure and safeguard financial stability. While a majority of central banks in emerging

East Asia kept their monetary policy rates on hold during the review period, Bank Indonesia raised rates unexpectedly by 25 bps on 19 October to support rupiah stability and avert further capital outflows from its financial market (**Table B**). The Bank of Thailand raised its policy rate by 25 bps on 27 September, following an earlier rate hike in August, as a preemptive move to contain inflationary pressure from supply-side factors, particularly the government's proposed economic stimulus measures. Likewise, the Bangko Sentral ng Pilipinas raised its policy rate by 25 bps in an off-cycle move on 26 October. Amid rising food and oil prices, some markets in the region saw an uptick in inflation in September and October (**Figure B**). While some central banks in the region have reacted or are reacting to the rise in inflation, the Bank of Korea has indicated that it may also raise its policy rate but largely to safeguard financial stability. Higher bond yields and expectations of an extended period of higher interest rates in major advanced markets drove up bond yields in most emerging East Asian markets, where both the 2-year and 10-year yields rose between 1 September and 10 November. The rise in yields in the region were capped somewhat toward the end of the review period following the FOMC's 1-2 November meeting over the possibility that the Federal Reserve may no longer raise policy rates. The exception was in Singapore which saw a decline in its 2-year and 10-year yields during the review period, as headline inflation was stable and its core inflation continued to decline.

Due to expectations that the Federal Reserve will maintain higher rates for an extended period, the US dollar slightly strengthened against most emerging East Asian currencies. The average depreciation for all regional currencies was 1.0% (simple) and 0.4% (GDP-weighted) between 1 September and 10 November (**Figure C**). The Laotian kip suffered the largest decline (−5.1%) on high external debt levels and inflation. The Indonesian rupiah fell by 2.9%, driven by capital outflows from its financial market during the review period. The Thai baht also weakened by 2.5% amid slow GDP growth of 1.5% y-o-y in Q3 2023, versus 1.8% y-o-y in the previous quarter, and a rising fiscal deficit. In contrast, the Philippine peso appreciated marginally due to an influx of remittances ahead of the coming holiday celebrations. The Cambodian riel also strengthened (0.9%), buoyed by central bank intervention to support financial stability.

# Box: The Bank of Japan's Unprecedented Decade-Long Monetary Easing and Recent Challenges Caused by the Ultra-Weak Yen

Haruhiko Kuroda's decade-long governorship at the Bank of Japan (BOJ) from March 2013 to early April 2023 marked an important milestone in Japan's unconventional monetary easing policy, which was initiated in 1999.[a] Over the past 25 years, the BOJ has implemented various unconventional monetary easing policies to overcome mild but long-standing deflation. These include a zero-interest rate policy (1999–2000), quantitative easing (2001–2006), comprehensive monetary easing (2010–2013), and qualitative and quantitative monetary easing (QQE) with yield curve control (YCC) (2013–present). The BOJ has become not only a pioneer in pursuing unconventional monetary policies but also a reference point for other central banks. Kuroda was renowned for being a bold monetary easing practitioner (Kowalewski and Shirai 2023a, 2023b). This box will provide a brief overview of the unconventional monetary policy measures the BOJ has undertaken over the past decade and highlight recent changes under the new governor, Kazuo Ueda. The impact of unconventional monetary easing on developments in domestic bond markets and the associated impact on exchange rates will also be explored.

## Unprecedented Scale of Monetary Easing Initiated Under Kuroda's Governorship

In January 2013, the Government of Japan, led by the newly elected liberal democratic party, and the BOJ jointly adopted the 2% price stability target, the first single numerical target adopted in line with global standards. Kuroda assumed the governorship of the BOJ in March 2013 and at his first monetary policy meeting the next month he implemented bold, unprecedented monetary easing known as QQE. The new policy featured the adoption of a monetary base control as the operational target, shifting away from the conventional policy rate (uncollateralized overnight call rate) control. The QQE's key aim was to achieve 2% inflation within about 2 years by emphasizing the size of monetary easing by using a monetary base. An annual increase in the monetary base in the range of JPY60 trillion–JPY70 trillion was set by purchasing Japanese Government Bonds (JGBs) worth about JPY50 trillion up to the maximum 40-year maturity, together with exchange-traded funds and Japanese real estate investment trusts.

Before QQE, Japan faced an overvaluation of the yen for an extended period, reflecting low inflation and the yen's safe-haven currency status similar to the Swiss franc. When economic recessions took place as, first a result of the Lehman shock in 2008 and then the East Japan Earthquake and nuclear power plant accident in 2011, the yen appreciated further, adversely impacting Japanese manufacturers. For most of 2010–2011, the exchange rate remained below JPY80 to USD1. This trend was finally reversed in late 2012 when the liberal democratic party won a landslide victory in the general election. Just before the election, the party had begun to stress the need for both a 2% price stability target and unlimited massive monetary easing to achieve the target. Therefore, the formation of a new government generated speculation among investors that massive monetary easing would be forthcoming under the newly elected BOJ governor in the following year.

The depreciation of the yen, together with higher economic growth in 2013, contributed to turning deflation to inflation and increasing long-term inflationary expectations—such as the inflation swap forward (5Y5Y) shifting from a negative rate in November 2012 to 1.0% by the middle of 2016. However, the increase in long-term inflationary expectations did not last long and began to decline from around mid-2014, partly due to the slowdown in economic growth caused by a consumption tax hike in April 2014 and partly due to a sharp decline in oil prices. The increase in the consumption tax from 5% to 8% boosted Japan's inflation by around 2 percentage points to about 4% and generated a substantial price shock, thus reducing household consumption and weakening economic growth. The combination of these factors led the BOJ to expand QQE in October 2014, while the yen depreciated to about JPY125 to USD1 by the middle of 2015 (**Figure B.1**).

In response to unfavorable economic conditions, the BOJ decided to accelerate the annual pace of expansion in the monetary base from JPY60–70 trillion trillion to about JPY80 trillion. To achieve this monetary base targeting, the amount outstanding of JGB holdings was increased through massive purchases of about JPY80 trillion annually. Purchases of exchange-traded funds and Japanese real estate investment trusts were also increased. This revision of the QQE parameters contributed to the further depreciation of the yen, but this depreciation did not translate into higher long-term inflationary expectations this time. In October 2014, the yield of the Japanese yen inflation swap forward (5Y5Y) was well above 1.0%; by early February 2015, it had

---

[a]   This box was written by Sayuri Shirai, an advisor for sustainable policies at the Asian Development Bank Institute, a professor at the Faculty of Policy Management of Keio University, and a former policy board member of the Bank of Japan.

*continued on next page*

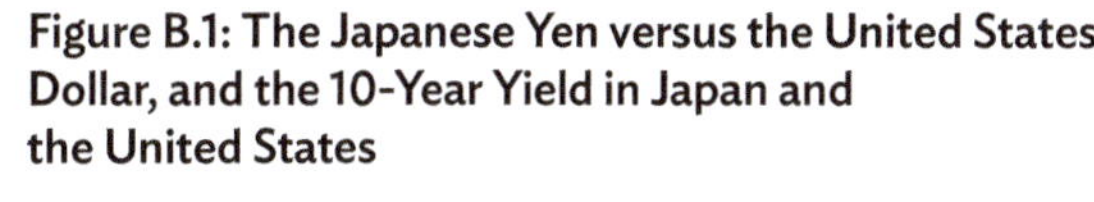

**Figure B.1: The Japanese Yen versus the United States Dollar, and the 10-Year Yield in Japan and the United States**

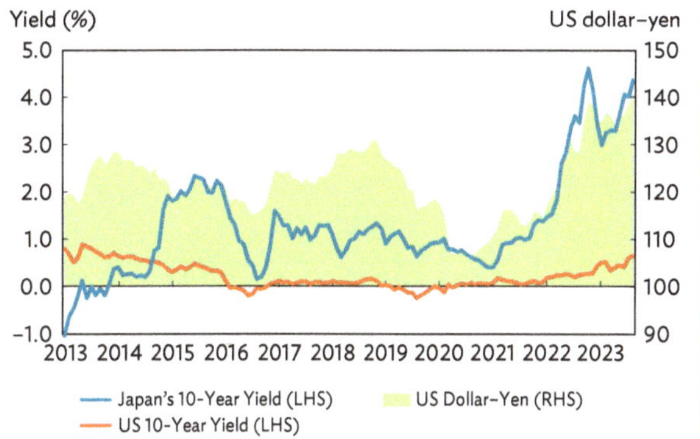



LHS = left-hand side, RHS = right-hand side, US = United States.
Source: Federal Reserve Bank of St. Louis. FRED Economic Data (accessed 10 June 2023).

fallen to slightly above 0.6%. In 2016, the BOJ became the fifth major central bank in the world to announce a negative interest rate policy, adding to the policy goals of QQE. The negative rate (–0.1%), however, was applied to only a small portion of the BOJ's current account balance. Adopting a three-tier system with the deposit interest rates of –0.1%, 0%, and 0.1%, the BOJ took every possible effort to minimize the damage of negative interest rates on banks' profitability.

**Yield Curve Control as a Turning Point in the Bank of Japan's Monetary Easing**

In September 2016, the BOJ introduced YCC, which sought to stabilize the 10-year yield at around 0% in conjunction with the negative interest rate policy. The YCC was a big leap from the QQE since the operation target was changed from the monetary base control to the two short- and long-term interest rates (i.e., –0.1% applied to part of the current account balance and 0% to the 10-year yield). The YCC concept reflected the experience of the United States (US), which set a cap on the yields of 10-year Treasury securities (2.5%) and 3-month Treasury bills (0.375%) during World War II to reduce government deficits driven by increased spending following the US' entry into the war. The BOJ aimed for the YCC to exert strong downward pressure on long-term interest rates and thus stimulate aggregate demand (Amamiya 2017). Meanwhile, market participants widely viewed that the switch to the YCC was undertaken for two reasons. One reason was to correct the tensions created in bond markets due to a substantial concentration of JGB holdings on the BOJ's balance sheet,

which accounted for almost 40% of all JGBs outstanding at that time. The resultant scarcity of JGBs reduced liquidity and the functioning of the JGB market. Another was a correction of the 10-year yield, which had fallen into negative territory (–0.25%) and generated negative returns for institutional investors (Figure B.1). The central bank found it increasingly challenging to meet the monetary base target by simply purchasing more JGBs. In addition, the rising scarcity of JGBs reduced liquidity and the functioning of the JGB market. The BOJ thus needed to find a new approach to switch from the quantity-based operational target (Shirai 2018). Under the YCC, the BOJ was able to reduce the amount of JGB purchases steadily and the 10-year yield remained low from 2016 to early 2022.

**The COVID-19 Pandemic, Yield Curve Control, and the Yen's Sharp Depreciation**

In the face of the coronavirus disease (COVID-19) pandemic, many developed economies took unprecedented monetary and fiscal measures in tandem to mitigate the adverse economic effects caused by lockdowns and mobility controls. While the Federal Reserve and the European Central Bank conducted massive asset purchases, the BOJ's reaction was rather muted in terms of such purchases. Instead, it launched new 1-year lending programs at 0% to foster banks' credit extensions to the private sector while maintaining the YCC. To promote banks' borrowing from the BOJ, the pool of eligible collateral was expanded. The interest rate applied to the BOJ's outstanding current account balances corresponding to the outstanding amounts of these loans was also raised to a range of 0.1%–0.2% to mitigate the adverse impacts of the negative interest rate policy and promote bank lending. This facility was terminated in March 2023.

Under the YCC, the yen–dollar exchange rate remained relatively stable and more or less fair-valued in a range of JPY105–JPY115 to USD1 for more than 5 years. This exchange rate development changed suddenly in 2022, when almost all central banks worldwide started to raise their policy rates to cope with rising inflation. By not raising its rates, the BOJ was the only exception among all developed economies. This interest rate divergence, supported by the YCC, was strong enough to generate substantial yen depreciation. The exchange rate exceeded JPY150 to USD1 briefly in October 2022 and has since reversed to around JPY130–JPY140 to USD1 with substantial fluctuations, mainly reflecting the decline in the 10-year yield in the US, Japan's Ministry of Finance's intervention in the foreign exchange market in September–October 2022, as well as the BOJ's

*continued on next page*

**Box**   *continued*

monetary policy adjustment pointed out below. The yen's undervaluation contributed to import inflation and sluggish consumption growth.

In late 2022, the BOJ expanded its tolerance band around the 10-year yield target from ±25 basis points (bps) to ±50 bps. This surprise move created substantial volatility in the JGB bond market, mainly because of the previous rejection of such a policy by the BOJ in September 2022. The decision was made for several reasons—primarily, to correct distortions and improve the functioning of the bond market. This policy adjustment contributed to a reversal of the depreciation of the yen and thus the yen appreciated to around JPY130 per USD1 by early 2023. The first 4 months of 2023 before the end of Kuroda's governorship confirm that this was a step in the right direction since the bond market's functioning improved moderately. Meanwhile, many market participants believe that the BOJ's surprise action was taken to cope with the yen's undervaluation.

The Japanese bond market has stabilized somewhat since February this year and issues observed in the world banking system caused by the collapse of Silicon Valley Bank and the Credit Suisse scandals did not cause particular tensions from the point of view of preserving the YCC framework. At the same time, the decade-long unconventional monetary experiments ended up expanding the BOJ's balance sheet significantly to JPY735 trillion at end-March 2023 from JPY166 trillion at end-March 2013 and JGB holdings to JPY576 trillion from JPY 91 trillion during the same period, accounting for 53% of outstanding JGBs (**Figure B.2**).

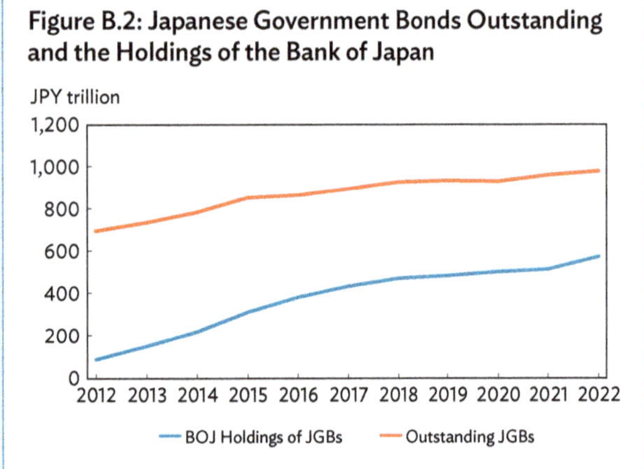

**Figure B.2: Japanese Government Bonds Outstanding and the Holdings of the Bank of Japan**



BOJ = Bank of Japan, JGB = Japanese Government Bond, JPY = Japanese yen.
Source: Prepared by the author based on Bank of Japan Flow of Funds (accessed 5 September 2023).

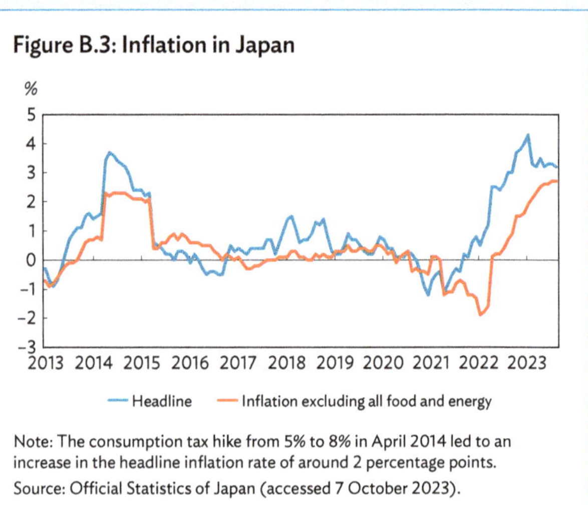

**Figure B.3: Inflation in Japan**



Note: The consumption tax hike from 5% to 8% in April 2014 led to an increase in the headline inflation rate of around 2 percentage points.
Source: Official Statistics of Japan (accessed 7 October 2023).

Over the past decade, Japan gradually moved away from deflation to moderate inflation, and inflation has been above the 2% price stability target since April 2022 (**Figure B.3**). The BOJ's monetary easing, in spite of the scale and various tools adopted, could not achieve the 2% inflation target except when the consumption tax hike in April 2014 briefly resulted in the rate of inflation exceeding 2%. Then, due to commodity price hikes and the depreciation of the yen, the rate of inflation again exceeded 2% in April 2022 and has remained above 3% since August 2022. However, this is mostly cost-push inflation. Currently, about 70% of inflation is due to food price hikes as government subsidies maintain low energy-related inflation. Another nearly 10% of inflation is due to an increase in hotel fees driven by a growing number of inbound tourists, which is partly a result of the sharp depreciation of the yen.

The BOJ has not declared victory, even though inflation has exceeded the 2% target for more than 1 year, since the contributing factors—such as commodity prices and the depreciation of the yen—are external in nature and likely to dissipate. The BOJ therefore maintains monetary easing because inflation is projected to decline toward the end of 2023 and may fall below 2% again in the foreseeable future. However, the likelihood of inflation returning to negative territory is low because of various supply-side factors such as labor shortages, rising production costs in the People's Republic of China (and the relocation of production to Japan and other countries as part of the de-risking process), climate change, and the Russian invasion of Ukraine.

*continued on next page*

**Box**  *continued*

It is yet to be seen how the policies pursued by the BOJ in the last decade will be evaluated in the future. Kuroda's legacy at the BOJ depends on how the BOJ's new governor, Kazuo Ueda, will treat his predecessor's policy. On this front, it is important to conduct a broad-perspective review of monetary policy covering a period of 25 years, which the new BOJ policy board promised to do within 1.0–1.5 years at its first monetary policy meeting in April 2023.

**New Challenges for the New Governor**

From the beginning, the new BOJ governor stressed the importance of achieving stable 2% inflation based on a virtuous demand-driven, wage-price cycle and the need to maintain monetary easing to do so. At the same time, the governor also pointed out the side effects arising from the YCC—such as distortions in the JGB market—and indicated that such side effect should be dealt with to sustain monetary easing if the BOJ finds that monetary easing will have to be maintained longer than it expects. While market participants expected the BOJ's actions toward normalization, the YCC was maintained at the April and June monetary policy meetings. However, the BOJ increased its flexibility in July by expanding the 10-year ceiling from 50 bps to 100 bps and by keeping 50 bps as the reference.

Since the yen has depreciated against the dollar by about 13% year-to-date in 2023, market participants widely view the BOJ's action as a response to mitigate the yen's excessive undervaluation and the subsequent cost-push inflation, which are hurting consumers and importers. There are no currencies among Japan's major trading partners that have depreciated since 2021 to the same extent as the yen (**Figure B.4**). The resurgence of yen depreciation since late May this year can be attributed to the BOJ signaling that it favors the current pace of monetary easing to achieve stable 2% inflation. The unexpectedly robust US economy, coupled with a services inflation rate (excluding energy) in the 5% range, driven by strong domestic demand and a tight labor market, suggests that there is little likelihood of an interest rate cut in the near term. The Federal Reserve may either raise interest rates once more this year or maintain the current rate until around the middle of 2024. Given this scenario, the BOJ's insistence on maintaining the status quo could benefit yen carry trades due to the stable interest rate differential. Hence, market participants view that the policy adjustment in July 2023 may have been deemed necessary to correct excessive yen depreciation.

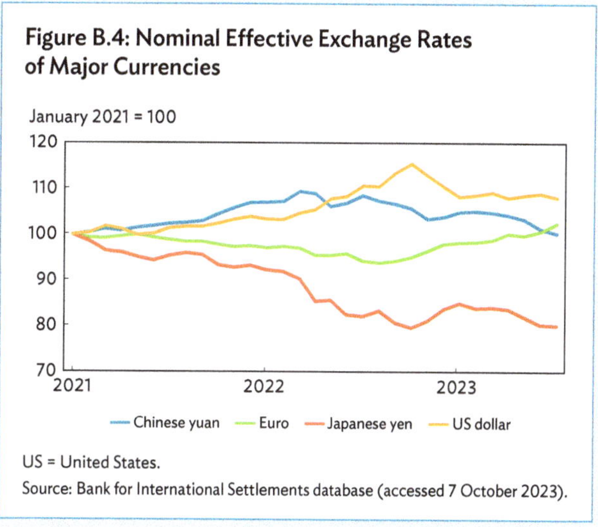


**Figure B.4: Nominal Effective Exchange Rates of Major Currencies**

US = United States.

Source: Bank for International Settlements database (accessed 7 October 2023).

The yen depreciated even further after this policy response because of the expectation that the interest rate differential between Japan and the US would remain large for an extended period. Meanwhile, market participants are increasingly expecting the BOJ to take more steps to normalize monetary policy by the end of next year, including the abolishment of negative interest rates and/or the removal of the 10-year yield target set at around 0% and the abolishment of the 10-year yield control. It is noticeable that the governor recently started mentioning the possibility of ending negative interest rates if the BOJ gains confidence that persistent inflation will be accompanied by wage growth. The market interpreted this as BOJ's efforts to correct excessive yen depreciation by hinting at the possibility of further policy adjustments toward normalization. Thus, the market is likely to continue exerting upward pressure on 10-year interest rates, testing the BOJ's resolve.

**Appropriate Steps for Normalization**

Finally, let us assume that the BOJ has decided to steer toward normalization, temporarily setting aside the agenda of achieving 2% price stability. In this case, the following sequence for normalization can be envisaged:

First, abolishing the 0.5% reference on 10-year interest rates and establishing a clear range with a 1 percentage point fluctuation margin could be pursued to enhance transparency. Next, eliminating the targeted 0% yield for the 10-year JGB could be examined since the 0% target is no longer binding and the reference rate currently has a more significant impact

*continued on next page*

**Box**   *continued*

on the prevailing 10-year yield. However, some market participants may interpret this action as another step toward normalization, potentially generating further upward pressure on the 10-year yield. Once the 10-year target is abolished, the next step could be the elimination of negative interest rates applied to part of the excess current account balance, while transitioning to 0%. As having both the 10-year interest rate and short-term interest rates at 0% does not seem desirable from a yield curve perspective, this sequencing is important.

As these steps are taken, it is likely that the volatility of the 10-year interest rate will increase. Furthermore, in the longer term, considering the future natural interest rate and price trends, the 10-year yield might rise above 1%. This reflects that the natural interest rate is expected to rise due to factors such as corporate green and digital investments, the drawdown of savings associated with the retirement of the baby boomer generation, and fiscal factors. In terms of prices, several factors—such as the increasing need for diversifying sources of production and procurement due to geopolitical risks, climate change, and wage increases due to labor shortages—will contribute to the likelihood of higher inflation compared to the period before the COVID-19 crisis.

Therefore, it is necessary for the government and businesses to prepare for a prolonged increase in long-term interest rates. Considering this, it might be appropriate to postpone the abolition of the 10-year interest rate fluctuation range until the public and investor understanding about the direction of monetary policy is strengthened through improved central bank communication.

Lastly, large Japanese companies increased regular wages by around 4% during this year's spring wage negotiations with labor unions, partly in response to the government's call for higher wages and the need to compensate for the rising cost of living. However, Japan's average nominal wage growth from April to August this year, including small and medium-sized companies, was only 1.6%. Average real wage growth remained negative at –2.2%. The BOJ hopes that wage growth may lead to the virtuous demand-driven, wage-price spiral. Currently, however, domestic demand remains weak partly because of negative wage growth. Inflation driven by strong consumer demand seems quite challenging at this stage, given the 2-decades-long period of wage stagnation, an increasing share of the elderly population relying solely on pensions, and expectations of tax hikes considering Japan's public debt. It is thus uncertain whether firms can achieve higher profits by raising productivity and offering higher wages to achieve positive real wage growth on a sustainable basis.

**References**

Amamiya, Masayoshi. 2017. "History and Theories of Yield Curve Control." Keynote Speech at the Financial Markets Panel Conference to Commemorate the 40th Meeting of the Bank of Japan, Tokyo. https://www.boj.or.jp/en/about/press/koen_2017/data/ko170111a1.pdf.

Kowalewski, Pawel, and Sayuri Shirai. 2023a. "History of Bank of Japan's More Than Two Decades of Unconventional Monetary Easing with Special Emphasis on the Frameworks Pursued in the Last 10 Years." Asian Development Bank Institute Working Paper No. 1380. https://www.adb.org/publications/history-of-bank-of-japan-s-more-than-two-decades-of-unconventional-monetary-easing-with-special-emphasis-on-the-frameworks-pursued-in-the-last-10-years.

———. 2023b. "A Quarter of a Century of the BoJ's Efforts to Overcome Liquidity Trap." *Bank i Kredyt* (Central Bank of Poland's Journal) 54 (4): 335–64. https://bankikredyt.nbp.pl/content/2023/04/BIK_04_2023_01.pdf.

Shirai, Sayuri. 2018. *Mission Incomplete: Reflating Japan's Economy*. Tokyo: Asian Development Bank Institute. https://www.adb.org/publications/mission-incomplete-reflating-japan-economy.

**Table B: Changes in Monetary Stances in Major Advanced Economies and Select Emerging East Asian Economies**

| Economy | Policy Rate 1-Nov-2022 (%) | Nov-2022 | Dec-2022 | Jan-2023 | Feb-2023 | Mar-2023 | Apr-2023 | May-2023 | Jun-2023 | Jul-2023 | Aug-2023 | Sep-2023 | Oct-2023 | Nov-2023 | Policy Rate 10-Nov-2023 (%) | Change in Policy Rates (basis points) |
|---|---|---|---|---|---|---|---|---|---|---|---|---|---|---|---|---|
| Euro Area | 0.75 | ↑0.75 | ↑0.50 | | ↑0.50 | ↑0.50 | | ↑0.25 | ↑0.25 | | ↑0.25 | ↑0.25 | | | 4.00 | ↑325 |
| Japan | (0.10) | | | | | | | | | | | | | | (0.10) | ◆ 0 |
| United Kingdom | 2.25 | ↑0.75 | ↑0.50 | | ↑0.50 | ↑0.25 | | ↑0.25 | ↑0.50 | | ↑0.25 | | | | 5.25 | ↑300 |
| United States | 3.25 | ↑0.75 | ↑0.50 | | ↑0.25 | ↑0.25 | | ↑0.25 | | ↑0.25 | | | | | 5.50 | ↑225 |
| China, People's Rep. of | 2.75 | | | | | | | | ↓0.10 | | ↓0.15 | | | | 2.50 | ↓ 25 |
| Indonesia | 4.75 | ↑0.50 | ↑0.25 | ↑0.25 | | | | | | | | | ↑0.25 | | 6.00 | ↑125 |
| Korea, Rep. of | 3.00 | ↑0.25 | | ↑0.25 | | | | | | | | | | | 3.50 | ↑ 50 |
| Malaysia | 2.50 | ↑0.25 | | | | | | ↑0.25 | | | | | | | 3.00 | ↑ 50 |
| Philippines | 4.25 | ↑0.75 | ↑0.50 | | ↑0.50 | ↑0.25 | | | | | | | ↑0.25 | | 6.50 | ↑225 |
| Singapore | – | | | | | | | | | | | | | | – | – |
| Thailand | 1.00 | ↑0.25 | | ↑0.25 | | ↑0.25 | | ↑0.25 | | | ↑0.25 | ↑0.25 | | | 2.50 | ↑150 |
| Viet Nam | 6.00 | | | | | | ↓0.50 | ↓0.50 | ↓0.50 | | | | | | 4.50 | ↓150 |

( ) = negative, ◆ = no change, – = no data.

Notes:
1. Data coverage is from 1 November 2022 to 10 November 2023.
2. For the People's Republic of China, data used in the chart are for the 1-year medium-term lending facility rate. While the 1-year benchmark lending rate is the official policy rate of the People's Bank of China, market players use the 1-year medium-term lending facility rate as a guide for the monetary policy direction of the People's Bank of China.
3. The up (down) arrow for Singapore signifies monetary policy tightening (loosening) by its central bank. The Monetary Authority of Singapore utilizes the Singapore dollar nominal effective exchange rate to guide its monetary policy.

Sources: Various central bank websites.

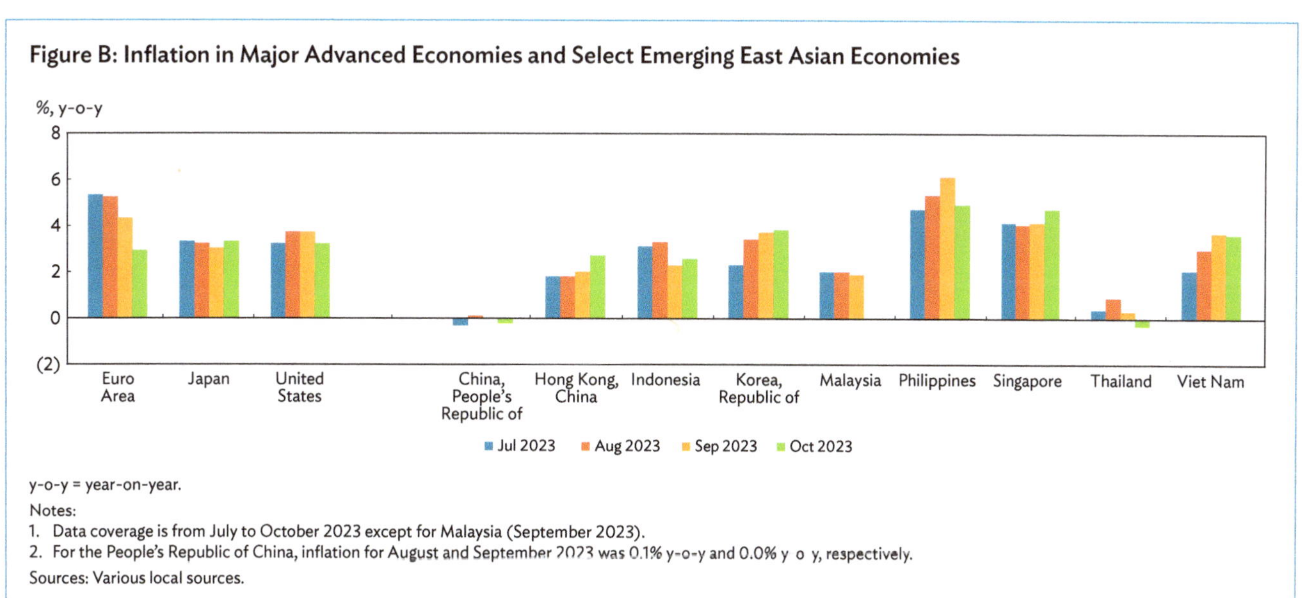

**Figure B: Inflation in Major Advanced Economies and Select Emerging East Asian Economies**



y-o-y = year-on-year.
Notes:
1. Data coverage is from July to October 2023 except for Malaysia (September 2023).
2. For the People's Republic of China, inflation for August and September 2023 was 0.1% y-o-y and 0.0% y-o-y, respectively.
Sources: Various local sources.

Figure C: Changes in Select Emerging East Asian Currencies versus the United States Dollar

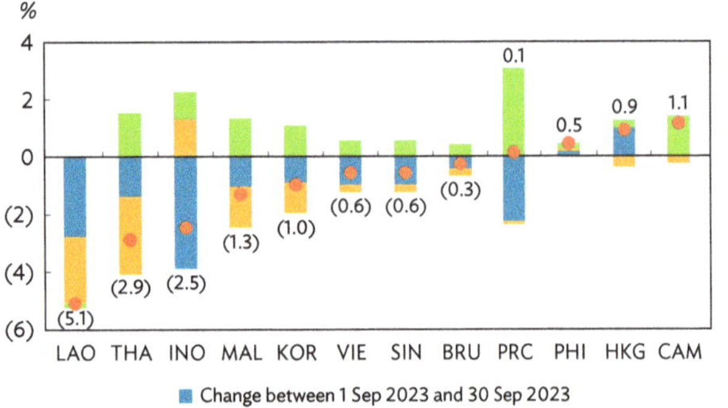



( ) = negative; BRU = Brunei Darussalam; CAM = Cambodia; HKG = Hong Kong, China; INO = Indonesia; KOR = Republic of Korea; LAO = Lao People's Democratic Republic; MAL = Malaysia; PHI = Philippines; PRC = People's Republic of China; SIN = Singapore; THA = Thailand; VIE = Viet Nam.

Notes:
1. A positive (negative) value for the foreign exchange rate indicates the appreciation (depreciation) of the local currency against the United States dollar.
2. The numbers above (below) each bar refer to the change between 1 September 2023 and 10 November 2023.

Source: *AsianBondsOnline* calculations based on Bloomberg LP data.

Gloomy economic outlooks in the region and globally, combined with negative investor sentiments amid expectations of higher-for-longer US interest rates, drove a retreat in most emerging East Asian equity markets and the widening of risk premiums across the region. The region's equity market dropped by an average of 4.9% (simple) and 4.3% (market-weighted) during the review period (**Figure D**). The largest equity losses were recorded in Thailand (−11.0%) and Viet Nam (−10.0%) over doubts about their respective economic prospects. Equity markets in the region posted further losses after the September FOMC minutes were released on 12 October, which indicated an extended period of elevated rates, and subsequently on 17 October over rising concerns about the current conflict in the Middle East. Regional equity markets, however, rebounded after the Federal Reserve left rates unchanged in its November FOMC meeting but the recovery was short-lived as hawkish speeches by some Federal Reserve officials on subsequent days dragged down sentiments in the region's equity markets. Risk premiums, as measured by credit default swap spreads, widened by 3.3 bps (simple average) and 1.4 bps (GDP-weighted average) during the review period (**Figure E**). In some markets, the risk premiums reflect market-specific uncertainties, including a weakened economic outlook. Credit default

Figure D: Movements in Equity Indexes in Select Emerging East Asian Markets

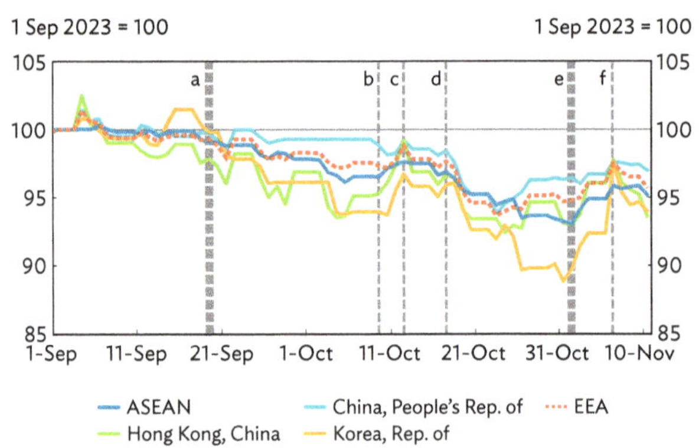



ASEAN = Association of Southeast Asian Nations, EEA = emerging East Asia, FOMC = Federal Open Market Committee, PRC = People's Republic of China, US = United States.

a Federal Reserve leaves rates unchanged and signals that it would keep interest rates elevated for a longer period.
b Dovish speeches from Federal Reserve officials.
c September FOMC minutes confirming higher interest rate for a longer period.
d Rising concerns over the current conflict in the Middle East.
e Federal Reserve leaves rates unchanged; notes that financial conditions have tightened.
f Hawkish speeches from Federal Reserve officials.

Notes:
1. ASEAN comprises the markets of Cambodia, Indonesia, the Lao People's Democratic Republic, Malaysia, the Philippines, Singapore, Thailand, and Viet Nam.
2. Data are as of 10 November 2023.

Source: *AsianBondsOnline* calculations based on Bloomberg LP data.

Figure E: Changes in Credit Default Swap Spreads in Select Emerging East Asian Markets (senior 5-year)

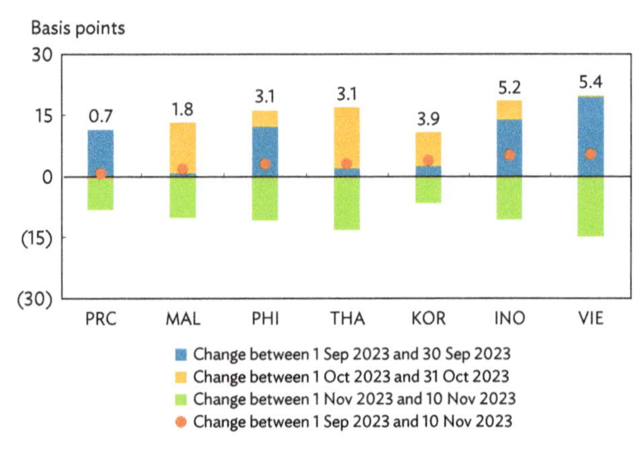



INO = Indonesia; KOR = Republic of Korea; MAL = Malaysia; PHI = Philippines; PRC = People's Republic of China; THA = Thailand; VIE = Viet Nam.

Note: The numbers above each bar refer to the change in spreads between 1 September 2023 and 10 November 2023.

Source: *AsianBondsOnline* calculations based on Bloomberg LP data.

swap spreads in Viet Nam and Indonesia widened the most in the region due to some weakness in their respective export sectors. Viet Nam also faces the risk of missing its 6.5% economic growth target for the year.

The Federal Reserve's signal of keeping interest rates elevated for an extended period dampened investor confidence in emerging East Asian capital markets, driving capital outflows. Regional equity markets experienced net foreign portfolio outflows of USD17.1 billion from 1 September to 10 November (**Figure F**). All markets in the region experienced outflows, with the People's Republic of China (PRC) accounting for the largest share, equivalent to USD11.3 billion, amid moderation in economic performances. The Republic of Korea also saw significant outflows of USD2.6 billion, reflecting the weak performance of the semiconductor industry, which faced a 32.6% decline in exports in the first 9 months of 2023 compared to the same period last year. Among Association of Southeast Asian Nations economies, aggregate net portfolio outflows amounted to USD3.1 billion, with Thailand registering the largest outflows at USD1.3 billion due to policy uncertainties under the new government. Meanwhile, the region's bond markets experienced foreign outflows of USD5.9 billion in September (**Figure G**). The PRC recorded the largest foreign bond outflows at USD1.8 billion in September, driven by

economic outlook concerns. In Indonesia, foreign bond outflows of USD1.5 billion were recorded in September when its reported Q2 2023 current account deficit added pressure to the rupiah.

Risks to the region's financial conditions remained balanced. On the downside, the Federal Reserve signaled it would keep interest rates higher for an extended period, which will lead to a longer period of elevated borrowing costs in most regional markets. Higher interest rates pose risks to borrowers with high leverage and liquidity needs to refinance their debts. For example, several high-profile property companies in the PRC have already experienced debt repayment difficulties. In economies where the banking sector has large exposure to these high-leveraged borrowers, the soundness of the banking sector and even the financial sector will be challenged. Similar liquidity stress is also present in the Lao People's Democratic Republic where the government needs to refinance its debt, a sizeable share of which is denominated in foreign currency. To safeguard financial stability, close monitoring of debt sustainability and liquidity conditions will be needed. Meanwhile, high interest rates will generally add to fiscal burdens, which may weaken fiscal conditions in some regional markets

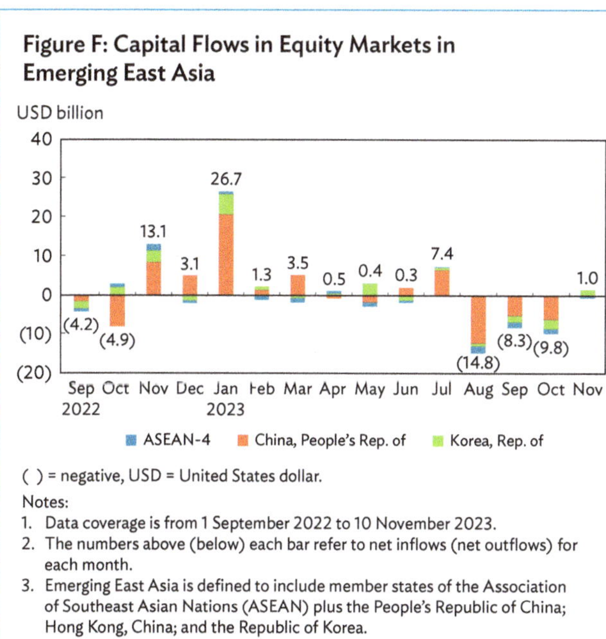

**Figure F: Capital Flows in Equity Markets in Emerging East Asia**

USD billion

( ) = negative, USD = United States dollar.

Notes:
1. Data coverage is from 1 September 2022 to 10 November 2023.
2. The numbers above (below) each bar refer to net inflows (net outflows) for each month.
3. Emerging East Asia is defined to include member states of the Association of Southeast Asian Nations (ASEAN) plus the People's Republic of China; Hong Kong, China; and the Republic of Korea.
4. ASEAN-4 includes Indonesia, the Philippines, Thailand, and Viet Nam.

Source: Institute of International Finance.

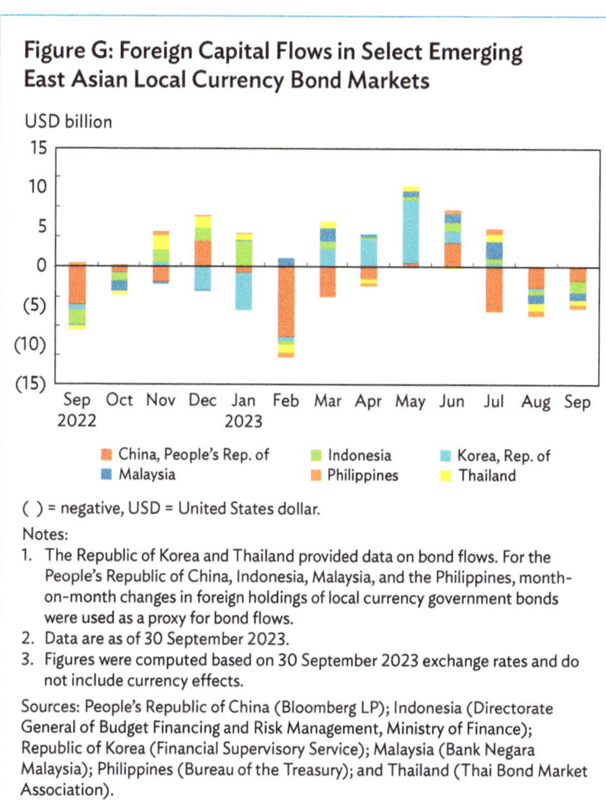

**Figure G: Foreign Capital Flows in Select Emerging East Asian Local Currency Bond Markets**

USD billion

( ) = negative, USD = United States dollar.

Notes:
1. The Republic of Korea and Thailand provided data on bond flows. For the People's Republic of China, Indonesia, Malaysia, and the Philippines, month-on-month changes in foreign holdings of local currency government bonds were used as a proxy for bond flows.
2. Data are as of 30 September 2023.
3. Figures were computed based on 30 September 2023 exchange rates and do not include currency effects.

Sources: People's Republic of China (Bloomberg LP); Indonesia (Directorate General of Budget Financing and Risk Management, Ministry of Finance); Republic of Korea (Financial Supervisory Service); Malaysia (Bank Negara Malaysia); Philippines (Bureau of the Treasury); and Thailand (Thai Bond Market Association).

even with sound fundamentals. For example, to support the economy, Thailand has introduced stimulus measures, while Indonesia increased its borrowing plans in the fourth quarter of the year. With higher interest rates, these measures become more costly, weakening the fiscal balance and possibly the local currency too.

On the positive side, inflation rates are largely expected to moderate next year, which, combined with headwinds to the regional economic outlook and heightened financial risks, could possibly ease the pressure of persistently high interest rates. While food and oil prices have risen and pushed up inflation recently, this is likely to be transient and inflation should decelerate next year, based on estimates in the recent *Asian Development Outlook*, and over the medium-term, according to Capital Economics Global Inflation Watch. Previous monetary tightening measures by regional central banks have yet to fully pass through and could also ease inflationary pressures. Moreover, various headwinds weighing on the regional economic outlook, including subdued global demand and a strained property market and weakened domestic demand in the PRC, together with looming financial risks from higher interest rates, may encourage central banks to consider ending their tightening stances to support economic growth.

# Bond Market Developments in the Third Quarter of 2023

## Section 1. Local Currency Bonds Outstanding

The emerging East Asian local currency (LCY) bond market posted annual growth of 8.2% in the third quarter (Q3) of 2023, reaching a size of USD23.5 trillion at the end of September.[3] Annual growth in the emerging East Asian LCY bond market continued to surpass that of the United States' (US) (8.1%) and the European Union 20's (EU-20) (6.1%). By the end of September 2023, the emerging East Asian LCY bond market was equivalent in size to 114.8% of the EU-20 bond market (USD20.5 trillion) and 62.8% of the US bond market (USD37.5 trillion) (**Figure 1**).

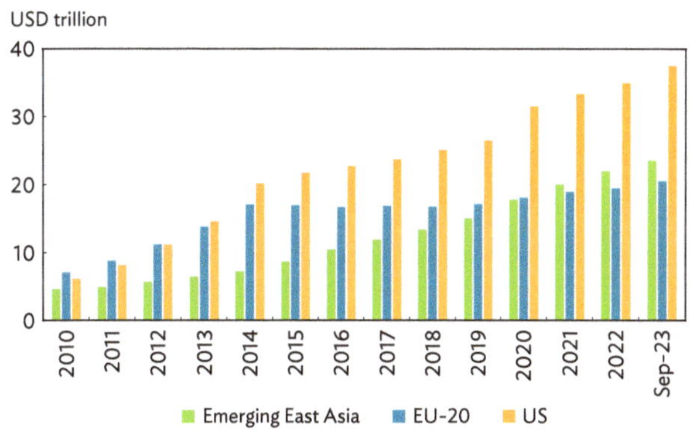

**Figure 1: Local Currency Bonds Outstanding in Emerging East Asia, the EU-20, and the United States**



EU = European Union, US = United States, USD = United States dollar.
Notes:
1. Emerging East Asia is defined to include the Association of Southeast Asian Nations plus the People's Republic of China; Hong Kong, China; and the Republic of Korea.
2. The EU-20 includes EU member markets Austria, Belgium, Croatia, Cyprus, Estonia, Finland, France, Germany, Greece, Ireland, Italy, Latvia, Lithuania, Luxembourg, Malta, the Netherlands, Portugal, Slovakia, Slovenia, and Spain.
Sources: People's Republic of China (CEIC Data Company); Hong Kong, China (Hong Kong Monetary Authority); EU-20 (Bloomberg LP); Indonesia (Bank Indonesia; Directorate General of Budget Financing and Risk Management, Ministry of Finance; and Indonesia Stock Exchange); Republic of Korea (Bank of Korea and KG Zeroin Corporation); Malaysia (Bank Negara Malaysia); Philippines (Bureau of the Treasury and Bloomberg LP); Singapore (Monetary Authority of Singapore, Singapore Government Securities, and Bloomberg LP); Thailand (Bank of Thailand); United States (Bloomberg LP); and Viet Nam (Vietnam Bond Market Association and Bloomberg LP).

All emerging East Asian LCY bond markets posted positive quarterly growth in Q3 2023, with growth in both regional government and corporate bonds outstanding picking up (**Table 1**). Growth in emerging East Asian outstanding government bonds rose to 3.0% quarter-on-quarter (q-o-q) in Q3 2023 from 2.4% q-o-q in the second quarter (Q2) of 2023, driven largely by accelerated sovereign and local government bond issuance in the People's Republic of China (PRC) aimed at supporting economic recovery. Meanwhile, growth in the region's LCY corporate bond market inched up to 1.5% q-o-q in Q3 2023 from 1.4% q-o-q in the preceding quarter (**Figure 2**).

**LCY bonds outstanding among members of the Association of Southeast Asian Nations (ASEAN) reached USD2.1 trillion at the end of September, accounting for 9.0% of the emerging East Asian aggregate.** Meanwhile, LCY bond markets in the PRC (USD18.7 trillion) and the Republic of Korea (USD2.3 trillion) accounted for 79.4% and 10.0% of the regional total, respectively. Government bonds comprised 62.4% of regional LCY bonds, totaling USD14.7 trillion at the end of September, followed by corporate bonds (USD8.3 trillion) and central bank bonds (USD0.5 trillion) accounting for 35.3% and 2.3%, respectively (**Figure 3**).

**The majority of LCY Treasury bonds in emerging East Asia have a remaining maturity of more than 5 years, limiting the impact of higher interest rates.** The region's Treasury bonds outstanding had a size-weighted-average tenor of 8.7 years at the end of September, with 53.7% of outstanding bonds carrying maturities of longer than 5 years. Across the region, the PRC; the Philippines; and Hong Kong, China had 52.4%, 53.8%, and 84.8%, respectively, of their outstanding Treasury bonds carrying maturities of 5 years or less at the end of September (**Figure 4**).

---

[3] Emerging East Asia is defined to include member states of the Association of Southeast Asian Nations (ASEAN) plus the People's Republic of China; Hong Kong, China; and the Republic of Korea.

## Table 1: Size and Composition of Select Emerging East Asian Local Currency Bond Markets

| | Q3 2022 | | Q2 2023 | | Q3 2023 | | | Growth Rate (%) | |
| --- | --- | --- | --- | --- | --- | --- | --- | --- | --- |
| | | | | | | | | Q3 2023 | |
| | Amount (USD billion) | % of GDP | Amount (USD billion) | % of GDP | Amount (USD billion) | % share | % of GDP | q-o-q | y-o-y |
| **China, People's Rep. of** | | | | | | | | | |
| Total | 17,676 | 104.8 | 18,325 | 107.4 | 18,675 | 100.0 | 109.2 | 2.5 | 8.4 |
| Treasury and Other Government | 11,510 | 68.2 | 12,122 | 71.0 | 12,440 | 66.6 | 72.7 | 3.3 | 10.9 |
| Central Bank | 2 | 0.01 | 2 | 0.01 | 2 | 0.01 | 0.01 | 0.0 | 0.0 |
| Corporate | 6,164 | 36.5 | 6,201 | 36.3 | 6,233 | 33.4 | 36.4 | 1.1 | 3.7 |
| **Hong Kong, China** | | | | | | | | | |
| Total | 350 | 96.9 | 366 | 99.6 | 385 | 100.0 | 103.0 | 5.1 | 9.7 |
| Treasury and Other Government | 30 | 8.3 | 30 | 8.1 | 37 | 9.6 | 9.9 | 23.2 | 22.2 |
| Government | 152 | 42.2 | 157 | 42.6 | 158 | 41.1 | 42.4 | 1.1 | 3.7 |
| Corporate | 168 | 46.4 | 180 | 48.8 | 190 | 49.3 | 50.8 | 5.6 | 13.0 |
| **Indonesia** | | | | | | | | | |
| Total | 377 | 30.3 | 409 | 29.9 | 399 | 100.0 | 29.8 | 0.5 | 7.2 |
| Treasury and Other Government | 344 | 27.6 | 376 | 27.5 | 366 | 91.9 | 27.3 | 0.5 | 8.0 |
| Central Bank | 3 | 0.2 | 4 | 0.3 | 4 | 0.9 | 0.3 | 6.8 | 23.9 |
| Corporate | 30 | 2.4 | 30 | 2.2 | 29 | 7.2 | 2.1 | (0.02) | (3.0) |
| **Korea, Rep. of** | | | | | | | | | |
| Total | 2,071 | 151.1 | 2,347 | 156.4 | 2,347 | 100.0 | 159.6 | 2.4 | 6.8 |
| Treasury and Other Government | 797 | 58.2 | 904 | 60.2 | 893 | 38.1 | 60.7 | 1.2 | 5.6 |
| Central Bank | 86 | 6.3 | 94 | 6.3 | 93 | 4.0 | 6.3 | 1.0 | 2.0 |
| Corporate | 1,188 | 86.7 | 1,349 | 89.9 | 1,361 | 58.0 | 92.5 | 3.3 | 8.0 |
| **Malaysia** | | | | | | | | | |
| Total | 400 | 124.8 | 419 | 126.7 | 422 | 100.0 | 127.5 | 1.5 | 7.0 |
| Treasury and Other Government | 225 | 70.4 | 239 | 72.3 | 240 | 56.8 | 72.5 | 1.1 | 7.9 |
| Central Bank | 0.9 | 0.3 | 3 | 0.8 | 3 | 0.8 | 1.0 | 29.2 | 273.5 |
| Corporate | 173 | 54.2 | 177 | 53.6 | 179 | 42.4 | 54.1 | 1.7 | 4.5 |
| **Philippines** | | | | | | | | | |
| Total | 190 | 52.6 | 212 | 50.4 | 210 | 100.0 | 50.2 | 1.8 | 6.5 |
| Treasury and Other Government | 157 | 43.4 | 175 | 41.6 | 171 | 81.3 | 40.8 | 0.3 | 4.8 |
| Central Bank | 7 | 1.9 | 8 | 2.0 | 12 | 5.7 | 2.9 | 44.8 | 65.4 |
| Corporate | 26 | 7.2 | 29 | 6.9 | 27 | 13.1 | 6.6 | (2.4) | 1.2 |
| **Singapore** | | | | | | | | | |
| Total | 450 | 101.9 | 504 | 105.7 | 512 | 100.0 | 107.9 | 2.6 | 8.2 |
| Treasury and Other Government | 160 | 36.2 | 180 | 37.7 | 183 | 35.7 | 38.5 | 2.8 | 8.8 |
| Central Bank | 167 | 37.8 | 198 | 41.4 | 204 | 39.9 | 43.0 | 4.4 | 16.5 |
| Corporate | 124 | 28.0 | 127 | 26.6 | 125 | 24.4 | 26.4 | (0.5) | (3.7) |
| **Thailand** | | | | | | | | | |
| Total | 411 | 90.4 | 459 | 91.7 | 455 | 100.0 | 92.9 | 1.9 | 6.9 |
| Treasury and Other Government | 227 | 50.1 | 257 | 51.4 | 256 | 56.3 | 52.3 | 2.3 | 8.6 |
| Central Bank | 67 | 14.7 | 67 | 13.4 | 67 | 14.8 | 13.7 | 3.1 | (2.9) |
| Corporate | 116 | 25.6 | 135 | 26.9 | 132 | 28.9 | 28.9 | 0.4 | 9.0 |
| **Viet Nam** | | | | | | | | | |
| Total | 98 | 25.3 | 108 | 26.0 | 109 | 100.0 | 26.6 | 3.9 | 12.5 |
| Treasury and Other Government | 66 | 17.0 | 78 | 18.9 | 77 | 71.2 | 18.9 | 1.5 | 19.0 |
| Central Bank | 1 | 0.3 | 0 | 0.0 | 4 | 3.6 | 0.9 | – | 208.6 |
| Corporate | 31 | 8.0 | 29 | 7.0 | 27 | 25.3 | 6.7 | (3.1) | (9.4) |
| **Emerging East Asia** | | | | | | | | | |
| Total | 22,024 | 101.0 | 23,148 | 103.2 | 23,514 | 100.0 | 104.9 | 2.5 | 8.2 |
| Treasury and Other Government | 13,517 | 62.0 | 14,360 | 64.0 | 14,664 | 62.4 | 65.4 | 3.0 | 10.3 |
| Central Bank | 486 | 2.2 | 532 | 2.4 | 548 | 2.3 | 2.4 | 4.2 | 8.9 |
| Corporate | 8,020 | 36.8 | 8,256 | 36.8 | 8,303 | 35.3 | 37.0 | 1.5 | 4.5 |
| **Japan** | | | | | | | | | |
| Total | 9,093 | 237.4 | 9,358 | 237.1 | 9,034 | 100.0 | 233.4 | (0.1) | 2.5 |
| Treasury and Other Government | 8,394 | 219.1 | 8,654 | 219.3 | 8,339 | 92.3 | 215.5 | (0.3) | 2.5 |
| Central Bank | 32 | 0.8 | 14 | 0.3 | 13 | 0.1 | 0.3 | (3.7) | (58.5) |
| Corporate | 667 | 17.4 | 691 | 17.5 | 682 | 7.6 | 17.6 | 2.2 | 5.6 |

( ) = negative, – = not applicable, GDP = gross domestic product, q-o-q = quarter-on-quarter, Q2 = second quarter, Q3 = third quarter, USD = United States dollar, y-o-y = year-on-year.

Notes:
1. For the People's Republic of China, Q3 2023 bonds outstanding data are based on *AsianBondsOnline* estimates. For Singapore, corporate bonds outstanding are based on *AsianBondsOnline* estimates.
2. GDP data are from CEIC Data Company.
3. Bloomberg LP end-of-period local currency–USD rates are used.
4. Growth rates are calculated from a local currency base and do not include currency effects. For emerging East Asia, growth figures are based on 30 September 2023 currency exchange rates and do not include currency effects..

Sources: People's Republic of China (CEIC Data Company); Hong Kong, China (Hong Kong Monetary Authority); Indonesia (Bank Indonesia; Directorate General of Budget Financing and Risk Management, Ministry of Finance; and Indonesia Stock Exchange); Republic of Korea (Bank of Korea and KG Zeroin Corporation); Malaysia (Bank Negara Malaysia); Philippines (Bureau of the Treasury and Bloomberg LP); Singapore (Monetary Authority of Singapore and Bloomberg LP); Thailand (Bank of Thailand); and Viet Nam (Vietnam Bond Market Association and Bloomberg LP).

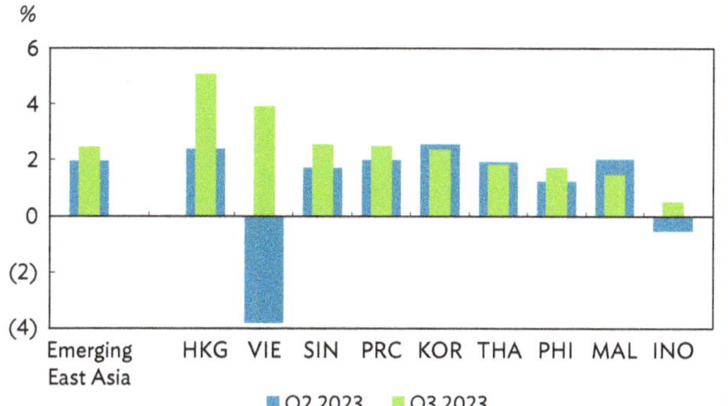

**Figure 2: Growth of Select Emerging East Asian Local Currency Bond Markets in the Second and Third Quarters of 2023** (q-o-q, %)



( ) = negative; HKG = Hong Kong, China; INO = Indonesia; KOR = Republic of Korea; MAL = Malaysia; PHI = Philippines; PRC = People's Republic of China; Q2 = second quarter; Q3 = third quarter; q-o-q = quarter-on-quarter; SIN = Singapore; THA = Thailand; VIE = Viet Nam.

Notes:
1. For the People's Republic of China, Q3 2023 bonds outstanding data are based on *AsianBondsOnline* estimates. For the Republic of Korea, Q3 2023 government bonds outstanding data are as of August 2023. For Singapore, corporate bonds outstanding are based on *AsianBondsOnline* estimates.
2. Growth rates are calculated from a local-currency base and do not include currency effects. For emerging East Asia, growth figures are based on 30 September 2023 currency exchange rates and do not include currency effects.

Sources: People's Republic of China (CEIC Data Company); Hong Kong, China (Hong Kong Monetary Authority); Indonesia (Bank Indonesia; Directorate General of Budget Financing and Risk Management, Ministry of Finance; and Indonesia Stock Exchange); Republic of Korea (Bank of Korea and KG Zeroin Corporation); Malaysia (Bank Negara Malaysia); Philippines (Bureau of the Treasury and Bloomberg LP); Singapore (Monetary Authority of Singapore and Bloomberg LP); Thailand (Bank of Thailand); and Viet Nam (Vietnam Bond Market Association and Bloomberg LP).

**Figure 3: Local Currency Bonds Outstanding by Economy and Type of Bond as of 30 September 2023**



ASEAN = Association of Southeast Asian Nations; HKG = Hong Kong, China; KOR = Republic of Korea; PRC = People's Republic of China.

Note: ASEAN comprises the markets of Indonesia, Malaysia, the Philippines, Singapore, Thailand, and Viet Nam.

Source: *AsianBondsOnline* calculations based on various local sources.

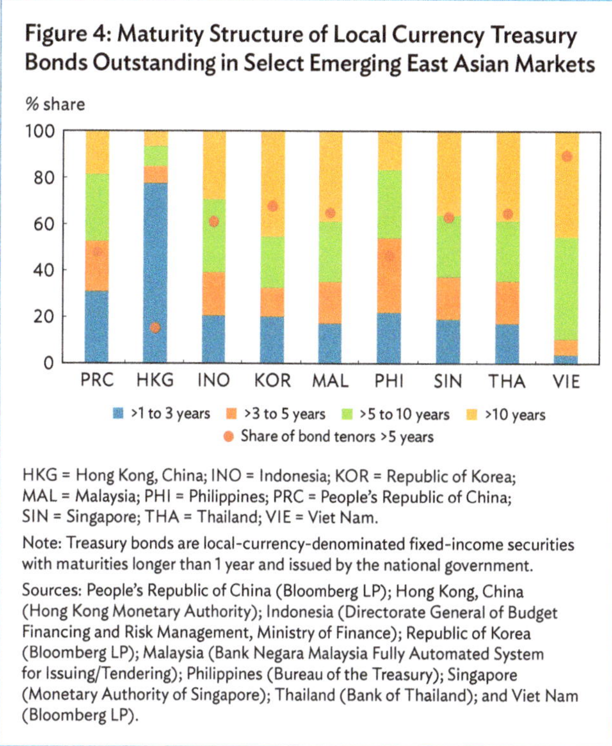

**Figure 4: Maturity Structure of Local Currency Treasury Bonds Outstanding in Select Emerging East Asian Markets**



HKG = Hong Kong, China; INO = Indonesia; KOR = Republic of Korea; MAL = Malaysia; PHI = Philippines; PRC = People's Republic of China; SIN = Singapore; THA = Thailand; VIE = Viet Nam.

Note: Treasury bonds are local-currency-denominated fixed-income securities with maturities longer than 1 year and issued by the national government.

Sources: People's Republic of China (Bloomberg LP); Hong Kong, China (Hong Kong Monetary Authority); Indonesia (Directorate General of Budget Financing and Risk Management, Ministry of Finance); Republic of Korea (Bloomberg LP); Malaysia (Bank Negara Malaysia Fully Automated System for Issuing/Tendering); Philippines (Bureau of the Treasury); Singapore (Monetary Authority of Singapore); Thailand (Bank of Thailand); and Viet Nam (Bloomberg LP).

**By the end of September, domestic investors held 89.4% of emerging East Asian LCY Treasury bonds.** Banking institutions, on average, held more than half of outstanding Treasury bonds in the region at the end of September (**Figure 5**). The largest shares of bank holdings were observed in the PRC (almost 70%) and the Philippines (nearly 50%). The major presence of banking institutions among investors in the PRC translated to the region's second-highest Herfindahl–Hirschman Index score, which is a measure of market concentration used to determine market competitiveness. Meanwhile, Viet Nam had the highest Herfindahl–Hirschman Index score in emerging East Asia as its market has only two dominant investors: insurance companies with a share of 59.7% and banks with 39.9%. Insurance and pension fund investors comprised a substantial share of investment in the Treasury bond market in Thailand (44.4%), Malaysia (33.3%), and the Republic of Korea (28.2%). Indonesia was the region's most diversified bond market at the end of Q3 2023, having the lowest Herfindahl–Hirschman Index score in emerging East Asia. For all investor types except banks (29.7%) and mutual funds (3.3%), the average market share was 16.7%. Indonesia was also the only market in the region whose central bank had substantial investor holdings (16.9%).

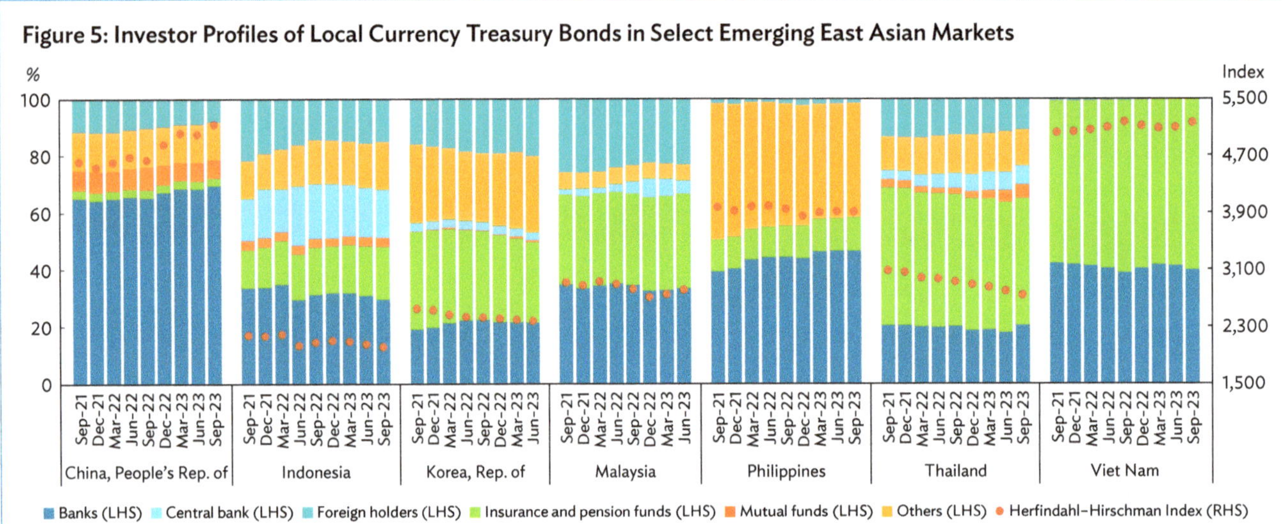

**Figure 5: Investor Profiles of Local Currency Treasury Bonds in Select Emerging East Asian Markets**



LHS = left-hand side, RHS = right-hand side.

Notes:
1. Data for the Republic of Korea and Malaysia are up to June 2023.
2. "Others" include government institutions, individuals, securities companies, custodians, private corporations, and all other investors not elsewhere classified.
3. The Herfindahl–Hirschman Index is a commonly accepted measure of market concentration. In this case, the index was used to measure the investor profile diversification of the local currency bond markets and is calculated by summing the squared share of each investor group in the bond market.

Sources: People's Republic of China (CEIC Data Company); Indonesia (Directorate General of Budget Financing and Risk Management, Ministry of Finance); Republic of Korea (Bank of Korea); Malaysia (Bank Negara Malaysia); Philippines (Bureau of the Treasury); Thailand (Bank of Thailand); and Viet Nam (Ministry of Finance).

# Section 2. Local Currency Bond Issuance

**LCY bond issuance in emerging East Asia accelerated to USD2.5 trillion in Q3 2023 on 8.6% q-o-q growth, almost doubling the 4.6% q-o-q expansion in Q2 2023.** Emerging East Asian LCY bond issuance in Q3 2023 was equivalent to 81.5% of that of the US (USD3.1 trillion) and was over three times that of the EU-20 (USD0.8 trillion) during the same period. The PRC, ASEAN markets, and the Republic of Korea comprised 65.1%, 19.7%, and 8.5% of total regional issuance in Q3 2023, respectively (**Figure 6**).

**Government bond issuance surged 13.2% q-o-q to USD1.1 trillion in Q3 2023, following a 2.3% q-o-q increase in Q2 2023, driven by higher issuance in the PRC.** Government bond issuance accounted for 43.5% of the regional total, with the PRC comprising 87.2% of the region's total government bond issuance (**Figure 7**). Issuance of government bonds in the PRC and ASEAN markets rose 15.5% q-o-q and 0.8% q-o-q, respectively. Meanwhile, government bond issuance in the Republic of Korea fell 12.9% q-o-q as the government had frontloaded its financing needs in the first half of the year. Central bank bond issuance rose 5.9% q-o-q in Q3 2023, driven by ASEAN markets.

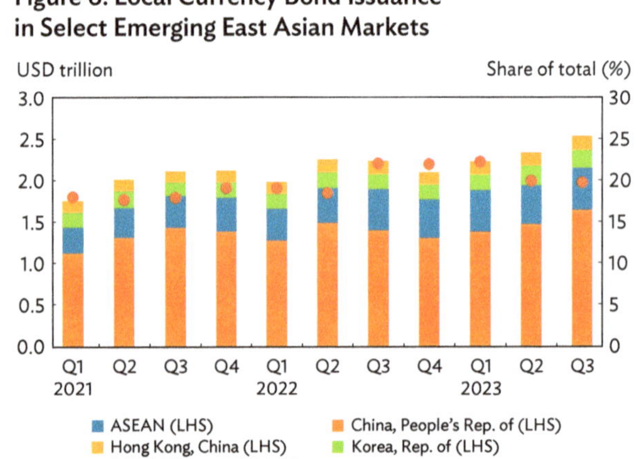

**Figure 6: Local Currency Bond Issuance in Select Emerging East Asian Markets**



ASEAN = Association of Southeast Asian Nations, EEA = emerging East Asia, LCY = local currency, LHS = left-hand side, Q1 = first quarter, Q2 = second quarter, Q3 = third quarter, Q4 = fourth quarter, RHS = right-hand side, USD = United States dollar.

Notes:
1. For the People's Republic of China, Q3 2023 bonds issuance data are based on *AsianBondsOnline* estimates.
2. ASEAN comprises the markets of Indonesia, Malaysia, the Philippines, Singapore, Thailand, and Viet Nam.
3. Figures were computed based on 30 September 2023 currency exchange rates and do not include currency effects.

Source: People's Republic of China (CEIC Data Company); Hong Kong, China (Hong Kong Monetary Authority); Indonesia (Bank Indonesia; Directorate General of Budget Financing and Risk Management, Ministry of Finance; and Indonesia Stock Exchange); Republic of Korea (Bank of Korea and KG Zeroin Corporation); Malaysia (Bank Negara Malaysia); Philippines (Bureau of the Treasury and Bloomberg LP); Singapore (Monetary Authority of Singapore and Bloomberg LP); Thailand (Bank of Thailand and Thai Bond Market Association); and Viet Nam (Vietnam Bond Market Association and Bloomberg LP).

**Figure 7: Local Currency Bond Issuance by Economy and Type of Bond in the Third Quarter of 2023**

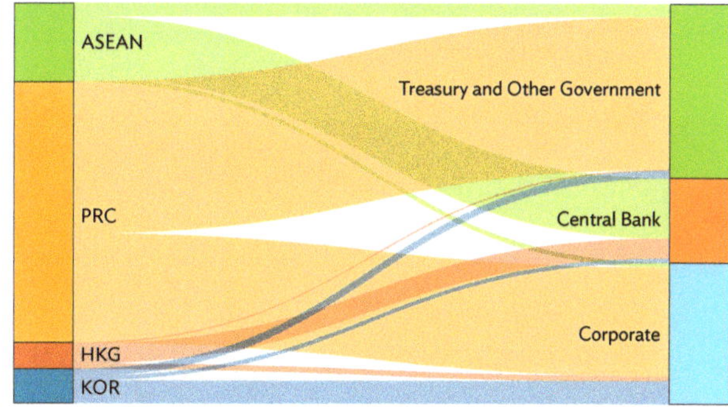



ASEAN = Association of Southeast Asian Nations; HKG = Hong Kong, China; KOR = Republic of Korea; PRC = People's Republic of China.

Note: ASEAN comprises the markets of Indonesia, Malaysia, the Philippines, Singapore, Thailand, and Viet Nam.

Source: *AsianBondsOnline* calculations based on various local sources.

**LCY corporate bond issuance totaled USD0.9 trillion in Q3 2023 on moderating growth of 5.0% q-o-q compared to 12.5% q-o-q in Q2 2023.** LCY corporate bond issuance accounted for 35.4% of total LCY bond issuance in emerging East Asia (**Table 2**). In four out of nine markets in the region, less corporate bond issuance was observed during the quarter due to high borrowing costs amid expectations that the US Federal Reserve would keep higher interest rates longer than previously anticipated. The PRC, the Republic of Korea, and ASEAN accounted for 77.0%, 16.0%, and 3.3% of the region's total LCY corporate bond issuance, respectively, on q-o-q growth of 6.5%, −3.8%, and −0.2%.

**The majority (55.6%) of regional Treasury bond issuance in Q3 2023 carried tenors of more than 5 years (Figure 8a).** In Viet Nam, the Philippines, and the Republic of Korea, over 80% of Treasury issuance carried maturities of over 5 years during the quarter (**Figure 8b**). The size-weighted tenor of Treasury bonds issued during the quarter marginally declined to 6.3 years from 6.7 years in Q2 2023.

## Section 3. Intra-Regional Bond Issuance

**Emerging East Asian intra-regional bond issuance inched up to USD13.8 billion in Q3 2023 from USD13.0 billion in Q2 2023 on growth of 6.2% q-o-q (Figure 9).[4]** Driven by the Republic of Korea, intra-regional bond issuance in Q3 2023 increased 75.5% from USD 7.8 billion in Q3 2022. Intra-regional bond issuance from the Republic of Korea increased more than eightfold in Q3 2023 from USD0.8 billion in the previous quarter. The next largest q-o-q gains in intra-regional bond issuance in Q3 2023 came from the Lao People's Democratic Republic and the PRC with growth of 89.7% and 73.3%, respectively. Meanwhile, in Hong Kong, China and Malaysia, intra-regional bond issuance decreased 39.1% q-o-q and 69.6% q-o-q, respectively. Hong Kong, China remained the region's largest issuer of intra-regional bonds with total issuance of USD7.1 billion in Q3 2023, accounting for 51.9% of the regional total. Among corporate issuers in the region, Hyundai Commercial, a corporate financing company domiciled in the Republic of Korea, issued a USD5.5 billion 2-year bond denominated in Chinese yuan, making it the single-largest issuance during the quarter and accounting for 39.8% of the regional total.

**CNY-denominated issuance and issuance from the financial sector dominated intra-regional bond issuance in Q3 2023.** CNY-denominated issuance equivalent to USD12.6 billion accounted for 91.9% of the regional total (**Figure 10**). Issuances denominated in Hong Kong dollars, Korean won, Singapore dollars, and Thai baht collectively accounted for 8.1% of the total intra-regional issuance in emerging East Asia. By sector, issuance from the financial sector comprised 69.7% of the regional total in Q3 2023 with aggregate issuance of USD9.6 billion, nearly three times the issuance of USD3.4 billion in Q2 2023. The transportation sector was the second-largest issuer of intra-regional bonds with USD1.4 billion (10.0% regional share), which was down from USD3.0 billion in the previous quarter. The utilities and real estate sectors, whose issuances increased during the quarter, were the third- and fourth-largest sources of intra-regional bonds in Q3 2023, respectively, accounting for 6.6% and 5.5% of the regional total.

---

[4]  Intra-regional bond issuance is defined as emerging East Asian bond issuance denominated in a regional currency excluding the issuer's home currency.

## Table 2: Local-Currency-Denominated Bond Issuance

| | Q3 2022 | | Q2 2023 | | Q3 2023 | | Growth Rate (%) | |
| --- | --- | --- | --- | --- | --- | --- | --- | --- |
| | | | | | | | Q3 2023 | |
| | Amount (USD billion) | % share | Amount (USD billion) | % share | Amount (USD billion) | % share | q-o-q | y-o-y |
| **China, People's Rep. of** | | | | | | | | |
| Total | 1,443 | 100.0 | 1,488 | 100.0 | 1,650 | 100.0 | 11.5 | 17.2 |
| Treasury and Other Government | 804 | 55.7 | 837 | 56.2 | 960 | 58.2 | 15.5 | 22.4 |
| Central Bank | 0 | 0.0 | 0 | 0.0 | 0 | 0.0 | – | – |
| Corporate | 639 | 44.3 | 651 | 43.8 | 689 | 41.8 | 6.5 | 10.7 |
| **Hong Kong, China** | | | | | | | | |
| Total | 160 | 100.0 | 156 | 100.0 | 168 | 100.0 | 7.8 | 5.1 |
| Treasury and Other Government | 6 | 3.9 | 1 | 0.8 | 7 | 4.4 | 515.8 | 19.4 |
| Government | 123 | 76.8 | 127 | 81.7 | 127 | 75.6 | (0.3) | 3.3 |
| Corporate | 31 | 19.3 | 27 | 17.6 | 34 | 20.0 | 22.9 | 9.0 |
| **Indonesia** | | | | | | | | |
| Total | 44 | 100.0 | 23 | 100.0 | 26 | 100.0 | 16.1 | (39.7) |
| Treasury and Other Government | 18 | 39.8 | 10 | 43.4 | 13 | 47.9 | 27.9 | (27.4) |
| Central Bank | 23 | 52.0 | 12 | 52.0 | 11 | 41.5 | (7.4) | (51.9) |
| Corporate | 4 | 8.3 | 1 | 4.6 | 3 | 10.6 | 168.3 | (22.6) |
| **Korea, Rep. of** | | | | | | | | |
| Total | 165 | 100.0 | 237 | 100.0 | 215 | 100.0 | (7.2) | 23.2 |
| Treasury and Other Government | 42 | 25.7 | 55 | 23.2 | 47 | 21.7 | (12.9) | 4.4 |
| Central Bank | 19 | 11.2 | 30 | 12.7 | 25 | 11.7 | (14.3) | 28.3 |
| Corporate | 104 | 63.1 | 152 | 64.2 | 143 | 66.5 | (3.8) | 29.9 |
| **Malaysia** | | | | | | | | |
| Total | 26 | 100.0 | 25 | 100.0 | 37 | 100.0 | 53.7 | 48.8 |
| Treasury and Other Government | 15 | 60.0 | 13 | 53.6 | 12 | 32.6 | (6.5) | (19.1) |
| Central Bank | 0.9 | 3.5 | 3 | 10.5 | 16 | 42.3 | 520.8 | 1,695.2 |
| Corporate | 9 | 36.5 | 9 | 35.9 | 9 | 25.0 | 7.2 | 2.2 |
| **Philippines** | | | | | | | | |
| Total | 49 | 100.0 | 39 | 100.0 | 42 | 100.0 | 9.6 | (17.0) |
| Treasury and Other Government | 18 | 37.5 | 10 | 26.3 | 10 | 24.6 | 2.5 | (45.5) |
| Central Bank | 28 | 58.2 | 28 | 70.7 | 31 | 73.7 | 14.3 | 5.2 |
| Corporate | 2 | 4.4 | 1 | 3.0 | 0.7 | 1.7 | (38.8) | (68.5) |
| **Singapore** | | | | | | | | |
| Total | 269 | 100.0 | 310 | 100.0 | 324 | 100.0 | 5.4 | 14.7 |
| Treasury and Other Government | 29 | 10.7 | 34 | 10.8 | 35 | 10.8 | 5.5 | 15.9 |
| Central Bank | 237 | 88.3 | 276 | 88.8 | 288 | 88.9 | 5.5 | 15.5 |
| Corporate | 3 | 1.0 | 1.2 | 0.4 | 1 | 0.3 | (17.3) | (66.1) |
| **Thailand** | | | | | | | | |
| Total | 59 | 100.0 | 70 | 100.0 | 61 | 100.0 | (10.0) | 1.0 |
| Treasury and Other Government | 16 | 26.9 | 18 | 25.5 | 15 | 24.0 | (15.4) | (9.8) |
| Central Bank | 28 | 48.0 | 35 | 49.8 | 33 | 54.0 | (2.3) | 13.8 |
| Corporate | 15 | 25.2 | 17 | 24.7 | 13 | 22.0 | (19.9) | (11.9) |
| **Viet Nam** | | | | | | | | |
| Total | 29 | 100.0 | 3 | 100.0 | 8 | 100.0 | 144.6 | (71.7) |
| Treasury and Other Government | 2 | 6.6 | 3 | 82.7 | 2 | 26.5 | (21.6) | 13.6 |
| Central Bank | 25 | 86.3 | 0 | 0.0 | 4 | 47.4 | – | (84.4) |
| Corporate | 2 | 7.1 | 0.6 | 17.3 | 2 | 26.2 | 269.0 | 4.3 |
| **Emerging East Asia** | | | | | | | | |
| Total | 2,243 | 100.0 | 2,352 | 100.0 | 2,532 | 100.0 | 8.6 | 13.4 |
| Treasury and Other Government | 951 | 42.4 | 981 | 41.7 | 1,102 | 43.5 | 13.2 | 17.8 |
| Central Bank | 484 | 21.6 | 510 | 21.7 | 535 | 21.1 | 5.9 | 7.2 |
| Corporate | 808 | 36.0 | 861 | 36.6 | 896 | 35.4 | 5.0 | 12.1 |
| **Japan** | | | | | | | | |
| Total | 373 | 100.0 | 380 | 100.0 | 378 | 100.0 | 3.1 | 4.5 |
| Treasury and Other Government | 347 | 92.9 | 349 | 91.9 | 340 | 89.9 | 0.8 | 1.1 |
| Central Bank | 0 | 0.0 | 0 | 0.0 | 0 | 0.0 | – | – |
| Corporate | 26 | 7.1 | 31 | 8.1 | 38 | 10.1 | 28.4 | 49.3 |

( ) = negative, – = not applicable, Q2 = second quarter, Q3 = third quarter, q-o-q = quarter-on-quarter, USD = United States dollar, y-o-y = year-on-year.

Notes:

1. For the People's Republic of China, Q3 2023 bonds issuance data are based on *AsianBondsOnline* estimates.
2. Data reflect gross bond issuance.
3. Bloomberg LP end-of-period local currency–USD rates are used.
4. Growth rates are calculated from a local currency base and do not include currency effects. For emerging East Asia, growth figures are based on 30 September 2023 currency exchange rates and do not include currency effects.

Source: People's Republic of China (CEIC Data Company); Hong Kong, China (Hong Kong Monetary Authority); Indonesia (Bank Indonesia, Directorate General of Budget Financing and Risk Management, Ministry of Finance; and Indonesia Stock Exchange); Republic of Korea (Bank of Korea and KG Zeroin Corporation); Malaysia (Bank Negara Malaysia); Philippines (Bureau of the Treasury and Bloomberg LP); Singapore (Monetary Authority of Singapore and Bloomberg LP); Thailand (Bank of Thailand and ThaiBMA); Viet Nam (Vietnam Bond Market Association and Bloomberg LP); and Japan (Japan Securities Dealers Association).

**Figure 8: Maturity Structure of Local Currency Treasury Bond Issuance in Emerging East Asia**

### a. Quarterly Maturity Structure

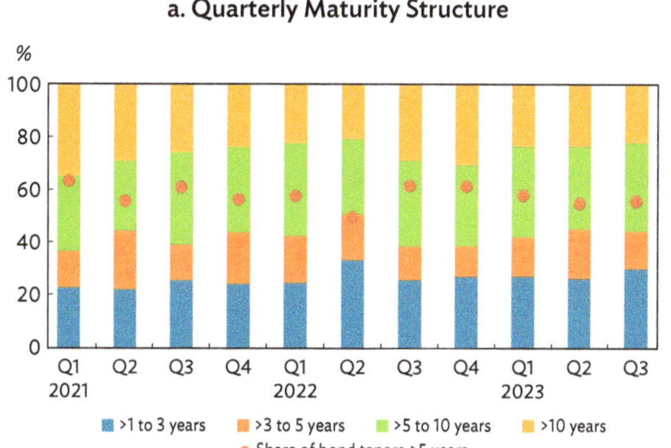


### b. Maturity Structure by Market, Q3 2023

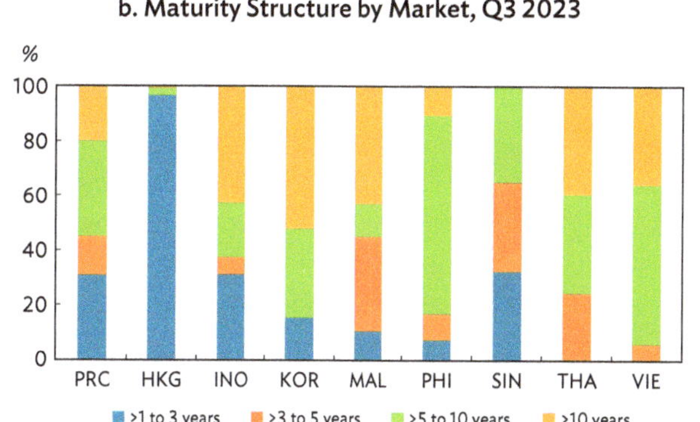


HKG = Hong Kong, China; INO = Indonesia; KOR = Republic of Korea; MAL = Malaysia; PHI = Philippines; PRC = People's Republic of China; Q1 = first quarter; Q2 = second quarter; Q3 = third quarter; Q4 = fourth quarter; SIN = Singapore; THA = Thailand; VIE = Viet Nam.

Notes:

1.  Figures were computed based on 30 September 2023 currency exchange rates and do not include currency effects.
2.  Treasury bonds are local-currency-denominated fixed-income securities with maturities longer than 1 year and issued by the national government.

Source: *AsianBondsOnline* calculations based on various local sources.

**Figure 9: Intra-Regional Bond Issuance in Select Emerging East Asian Economies**

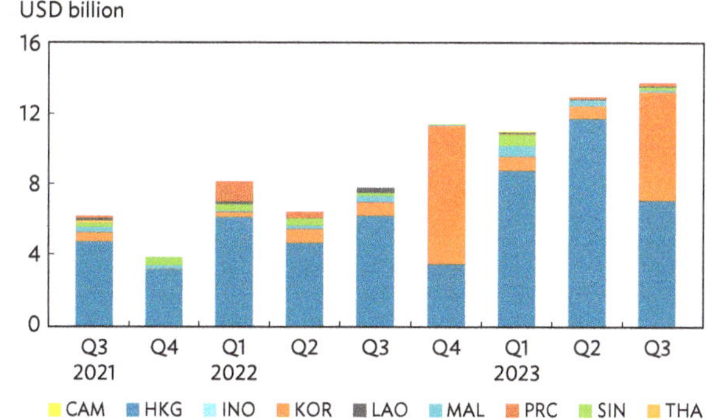


CAM = Cambodia; HKG = Hong Kong, China; INO = Indonesia; KOR = Republic of Korea; LAO = Lao People's Democratic Republic; MAL = Malaysia; PRC = People's Republic of China; Q1 = first quarter; Q2 = second quarter; Q3 = third quarter; Q4 = fourth quarter; SIN = Singapore; THA = Thailand; USD = United States dollar.

Source: *AsianBondsOnline* calculations based on Bloomberg LP data.

**Figure 10: Intra-Regional Bond Issuance in Emerging East Asia by Economy, Currency, and Sector in the Third Quarter of 2023**

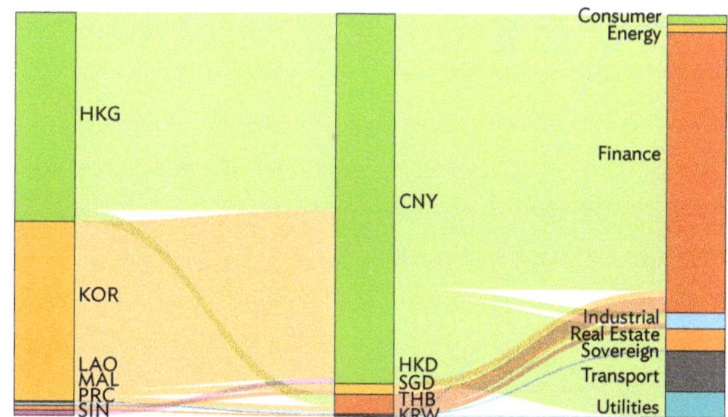


CNY = Chinese yuan; HKD = Hong Kong dollar; HKG = Hong Kong, China; KOR = Republic of Korea; KRW = Korean won; LAO = Lao People's Democratic Republic; MAL = Malaysia; PRC = People's Republic of China; SGD = Singapore dollar; SIN = Singapore; THB = Thai baht.

Source: *AsianBondsOnline* calculations based on Bloomberg LP data.

# Section 4. G3 Currency Bond Issuance

**G3 currency bond issuance in emerging East Asia reached USD41.1 billion in Q3 2023, up 10.2% from the USD37.3 billion issued in Q2 2023 (Figure 11).** However, this was 11.7% lower than total quarterly issuance a year earlier as USD-denominated issuances, representing 91.9% of the region's G3 currency bond issuance in Q3 2023, declined 13.3% y-o-y. The PRC regained its position as the largest issuer of G3 currency bonds in emerging East Asia during the quarter. Issuance of G3 currency bonds from ASEAN markets contracted 11.1% q-o-q to USD6.4 billion, accounting for 15.5% of the regional total (**Figure 12**). Malaysia and Singapore posted the largest G3 currency bond issuances among ASEAN markets, issuing USD2.4 billion and USD1.6 billion, respectively, while no G3 currency bonds were issued in the markets of Cambodia, the Lao People's Democratic Republic, the Philippines, and Viet Nam.

# Section 5. Yield Curve Movements

**From 1 September to 10 November, bond yield curves rose for nearly all markets in emerging East Asia.** Yields gained following the rise in US yields after the Federal Reserve indicated that it would hold interest rates elevated for longer than previously indicated. In addition, the region is seeing an uptick in inflation amid signs that commodity prices are increasing (**Figure 13**).

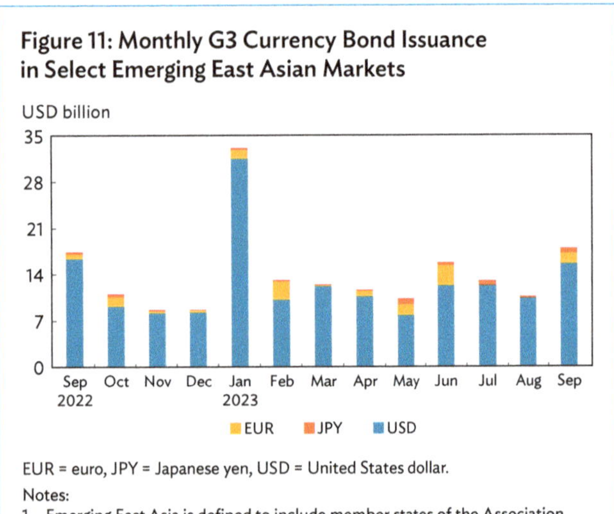

**Figure 11: Monthly G3 Currency Bond Issuance in Select Emerging East Asian Markets**



EUR = euro, JPY = Japanese yen, USD = United States dollar.

Notes:
1. Emerging East Asia is defined to include member states of the Association of Southeast Asian Nations (ASEAN) plus the People's Republic of China; Hong Kong, China; and the Republic of Korea.
2. G3 currency bonds are denominated in either euros, Japanese yen, or United States dollars.
3. Figures were computed based on 30 September 2023 currency exchange rates and do not include currency effects.

Source: *AsianBondsOnline* calculations based on Bloomberg LP data.

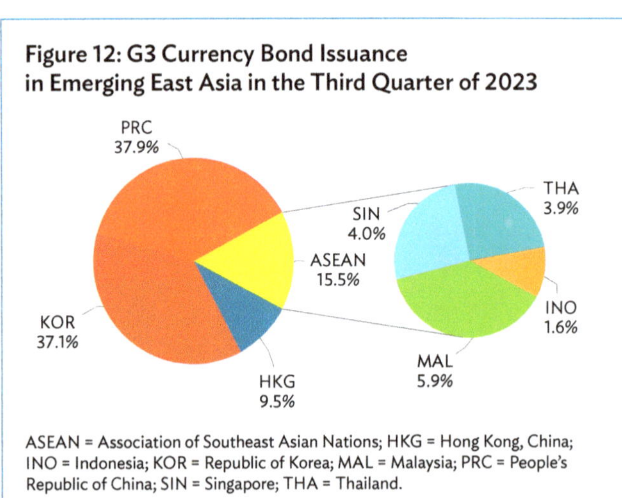

**Figure 12: G3 Currency Bond Issuance in Emerging East Asia in the Third Quarter of 2023**



ASEAN = Association of Southeast Asian Nations; HKG = Hong Kong, China; INO = Indonesia; KOR = Republic of Korea; MAL = Malaysia; PRC = People's Republic of China; SIN = Singapore; THA = Thailand.

Note: G3 currency bonds are denominated in either euros, Japanese yen, or United States dollars.

Source: *AsianBondsOnline* calculations based on Bloomberg LP data.

## Figure 13: Benchmark Yield Curves—Local Currency Government Bonds

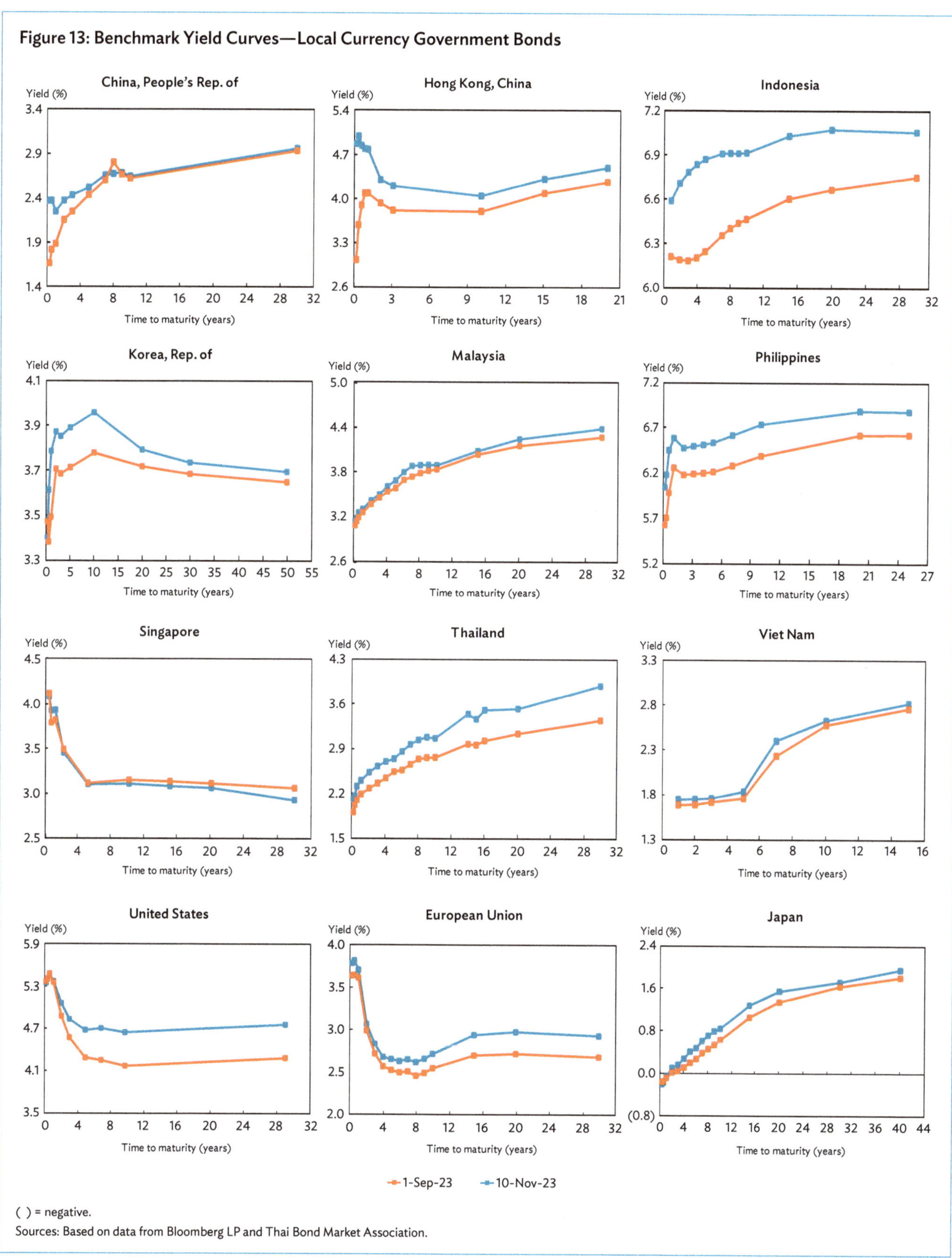



( ) = negative.

Sources: Based on data from Bloomberg LP and Thai Bond Market Association.

# Recent Developments in ASEAN+3 Sustainable Bond Markets

**Sustainable bonds outstanding in ASEAN+3 markets climbed to USD734.1 billion at the end of September, buoyed by robust issuance in the third quarter (Q3).**[5] The regional sustainable bond market expanded 33.6% year-on-year and 5.2% quarter-on-quarter (q-o-q) in Q3 2023, up from the 31.3% year-on-year and 5.0% q-o-q hikes posted in the second quarter (Q2) of 2023. The 5.2% q-o-q growth in Q3 2023 was the fastest q-o-q expansion among major regional sustainable bond markets around the world and surpassed the European Union's (EU-20) 2.6% q-o-q growth. This was largely fueled by ASEAN+3's sustainable bond issuance of USD57.3 billion in Q3 2023, which topped all other regions during the quarter. However, the EU-20 continues to be the world's largest sustainable bond market, accounting for 37.1% of the global sustainable bonds outstanding at the end of September, followed by ASEAN+3 at 18.9% (**Figure 14**). Despite its continued expansion, ASEAN+3's sustainable bond market only comprised 2.0% of the region's general bond market, lagging the EU-20's corresponding share of 6.7%.

**Sustainable bond markets in ASEAN+3 and the EU-20 are dominated by green bonds and local currency (LCY) financing.** ASEAN+3's sustainable bond market largely comprises green bonds (63.6%) and LCY financing (65.6%) (**Figure 15**). In the EU-20, green bonds account for a similar share (63.2%), while LCY financing is even more prevalent (89.9%). In terms of average maturity, however, ASEAN+3's sustainable bond market is dominated by short-term financing, with bonds carrying

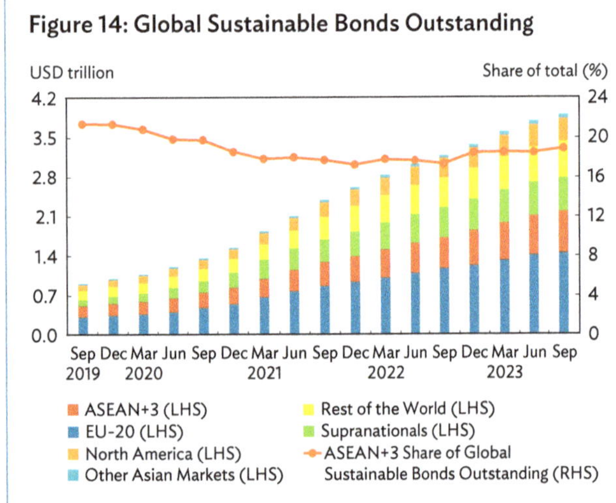

**Figure 14: Global Sustainable Bonds Outstanding**



ASEAN+3 = Association of Southeast Asian Nations plus the People's Republic of China; Hong Kong, China; Japan; and the Republic of Korea; EU = European Union; LHS = left-hand side; RHS = right-hand side; USD = United States dollar.

Notes:
1. EU-20 includes EU member markets Austria, Belgium, Croatia, Cyprus, Estonia, Finland, France, Germany, Greece, Ireland, Italy, Latvia, Lithuania, Luxembourg, Malta, the Netherlands, Portugal, Slovakia, Slovenia, and Spain.
2. Data include both local currency and foreign currency issues.

Source: *AsianBondsOnline* calculations based on Bloomberg LP data.

**Figure 15: Market Profile of Outstanding ASEAN+3 Sustainable Bonds at the End of September 2023**

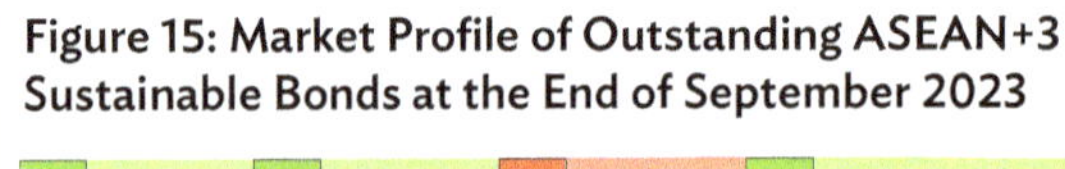

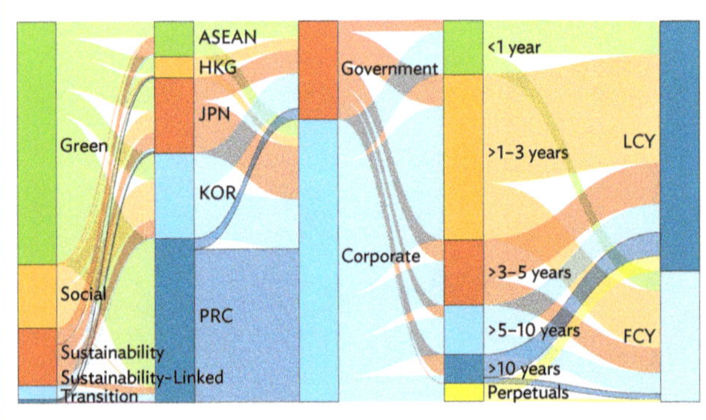



ASEAN = Association of Southeast Asian Nations; FCY = foreign currency; HKG = Hong Kong, China; JPN = Japan; KOR = Republic of Korea; LCY = local currency; PRC = People's Republic of China.

Notes:
1. ASEAN+3 is defined to include member states of the Association of Southeast Asian Nations (ASEAN) plus the People's Republic of China; Hong Kong, China; Japan; and the Republic of Korea.
2. ASEAN comprises the markets of Cambodia, Indonesia, the Lao People's Democratic Republic, Malaysia, the Philippines, Singapore, Thailand, and Viet Nam.

Source: *AsianBondsOnline* calculations based on Bloomberg LP data.

---

[5] ASEAN+3 is defined to include member states of the Association of Southeast Asian Nations (ASEAN) plus the People's Republic of China; Hong Kong, China; Japan; and the Republic of Korea.

maturities of 5 years or less accounting for 74.8% of total outstanding sustainable bonds at the end of September, while the average maturity of the EU-20's sustainable bond stock is much longer, with bonds with maturities of more than 5 years accounting for 60.2% of the total (**Figure 16**). At the end of September, the weighted average tenor in the ASEAN+3 sustainable bond market stood at 4.5 years compared with 8.6 years for the EU-20 market. This highlights the need for further policy actions and initiatives to expand ASEAN+3's sustainable bond market by increasing LCY financing and long-term financing.

**ASEAN+3 sustainable bond issuance remained strong despite headwinds in global financial markets.** Total sustainable bond issuance reached USD57.3 billion during Q3 2023, the most issuance among all regional sustainable bond markets during the quarter and accounting for 36.3% of the global total, though this was less than USD69.2 billion of issuance in Q2 2023 (**Figure 17**). Q3 2023 issuance of sustainability and sustainability-linked bonds rose 53.2% and 124.1%, repsectively, from the prior quarter, led by issuances from Japan, the People's Republic of China, and the Republic of Korea. In Q3 2023, Japan was the largest

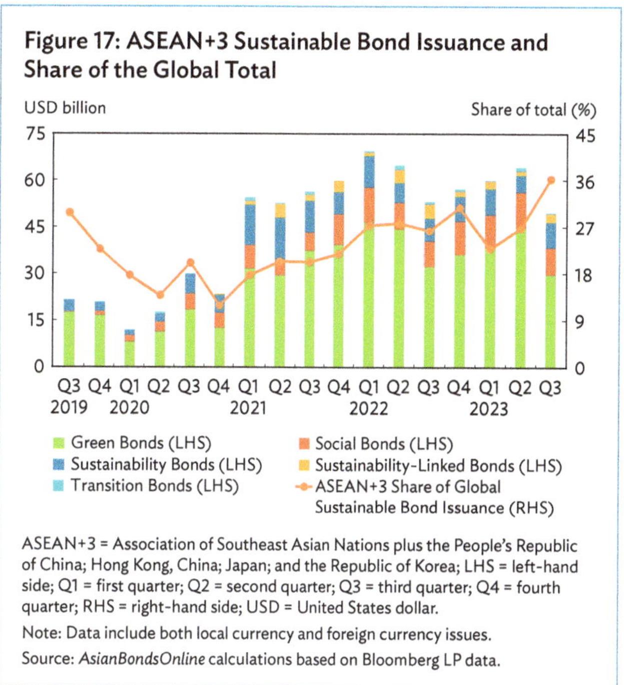

**Figure 17: ASEAN+3 Sustainable Bond Issuance and Share of the Global Total**



ASEAN+3 = Association of Southeast Asian Nations plus the People's Republic of China; Hong Kong, China; Japan; and the Republic of Korea; LHS = left-hand side; Q1 = first quarter; Q2 = second quarter; Q3 = third quarter; Q4 = fourth quarter; RHS = right-hand side; USD = United States dollar.

Note: Data include both local currency and foreign currency issues.

Source: *AsianBondsOnline* calculations based on Bloomberg LP data.

issuer of sustainable bonds in the region, accounting for 36.5% of the ASEAN+3 total, and up from its share of 20.2% in Q2 2023. ASEAN's contribution to the regional issuance total climbed to 7.4% in Q3 2023 from 4.6% in Q2 2023 and was much larger than its 2.3% share in ASEAN+3's general bond market during the quarter. ASEAN sustainable bond issuance climbed 32.7% q-o-q in Q3 2023, buoyed by government issuances from Singapore and Thailand. In August, the Government of Singapore raised SGD2.8 billion from the sale of 50-year green bonds. The Governments of Thailand and, to a lesser extent, Indonesia both included auctions for sustainable bonds in their scheduled Treasury auctions.

**Sustainable bond issuance in ASEAN+3 is dominated by LCY-denominated issuance, representing 69.5% of the total issuance during Q3 2023 (Figure 18).** The share of LCY financing in the ASEAN+3 sustainable bond market still lags that in ASEAN+3's general bond market (95.8%) and the EU-20's sustainable bond market (85.8%). This suggests that ASEAN+3's sustainable bond market needs further development to facilitate more LCY financing. During the quarter, however, all sustainable bond issuances in ASEAN markets were denominated in domestic currencies. In contrast, Hong Kong, China had 60.6% of its sustainable bond issuance denominated in foreign currency during the quarter.

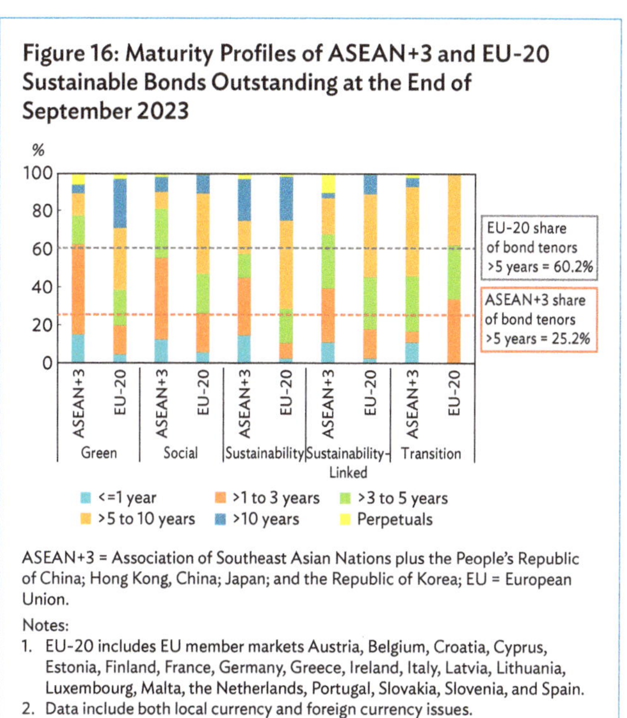

**Figure 16: Maturity Profiles of ASEAN+3 and EU-20 Sustainable Bonds Outstanding at the End of September 2023**



ASEAN+3 = Association of Southeast Asian Nations plus the People's Republic of China; Hong Kong, China; Japan; and the Republic of Korea; EU = European Union.

Notes:
1. EU-20 includes EU member markets Austria, Belgium, Croatia, Cyprus, Estonia, Finland, France, Germany, Greece, Ireland, Italy, Latvia, Lithuania, Luxembourg, Malta, the Netherlands, Portugal, Slovakia, Slovenia, and Spain.
2. Data include both local currency and foreign currency issues.

Source: *AsianBondsOnline* calculations based on Bloomberg LP data.

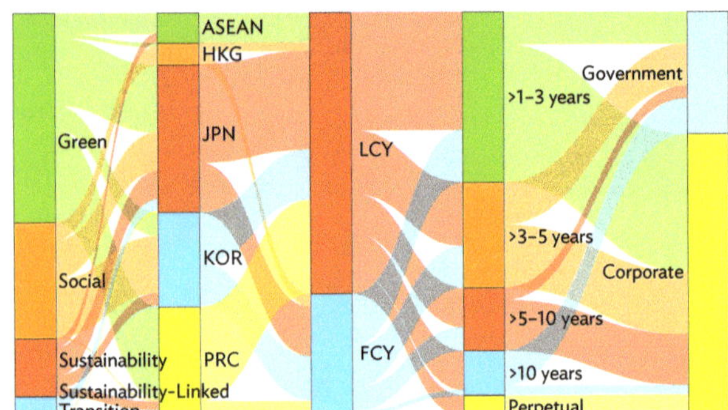

**Figure 18: Market Profile of ASEAN+3 Sustainable Bond Issuance in the Third Quarter of 2023**



ASEAN = Association of Southeast Asian Nations; FCY = foreign currency; HKG = Hong Kong, China; JPN = Japan; KOR = Republic of Korea; LCY = local currency; PRC = People's Republic of China.

Notes:
1.  ASEAN+3 is defined to include member states of ASEAN plus the People's Republic of China; Hong Kong, China; Japan; and the Republic of Korea.
2.  ASEAN comprises the markets of Indonesia, Malaysia, the Philippines, Singapore, Thailand, and Viet Nam.

Source: *AsianBondsOnline* calculations based on Bloomberg LP data.

**Short-term and private sector issuances were more prevalent in the ASEAN+3 sustainable bond market in Q3 2023.** 68.1% of all sustainable bond issuance in Q3 2023 had tenors of 5 years or less, with 42.1% carrying maturities of 3 years or less. In contrast, 65.1% of EU-20 sustainable bond issuance during the quarter had tenors of over 5 years. With Singapore's issuance of a SGD2.8 billion bond with a 50-year tenor, the weighted-average tenor of ASEAN+3 sustainable bond issuance in Q3 2023 was 7.2 years, which was broadly comparable with 7.6 years for the EU-20 market. Meanwhile, private sector issuance accounted for 69.8% of ASEAN+3 sustainable bond issuance during the quarter, much higher than the corresponding share of 33.1% in ASEAN+3's general bond market. ASEAN markets demonstrated a different pattern, with 81.5% and 88.5% of sustainable bond issuance in Q3 2023 coming from the public sector and comprising tenors of over 5 years, respectively.

# Policy and Regulatory Developments

## People's Republic of China

### The People's Bank of China Cuts Reserve Requirement Ratio

On 14 September, the People's Bank of China announced that it would cut the reserve requirement ratio of financial institutions by 25 basis points, effective 15 September. The central bank estimated that the move would reduce the weighted average reserve requirement ratio of financial institutions to 7.4%.

### The People's Republic of China Announces CNY1.0 trillion of Special Bond Issuance

On 25 October, the People's Republic of China announced that it would issue an additional CNY1.0 trillion of government bonds to help support fiscal stimulus measures. Under the plan, the proceeds of the government bonds will be transferred to local government units. In addition, the government raised its budget deficit target for 2023 from 3.0% to 3.8%.

## Hong Kong, China

### Hong Kong Monetary Authority Announces Government Bond Issuance Schedule

On 16 October, the Hong Kong Monetary Authority announced the tentative issuance schedule for Hong Kong Special Administrative Region government bonds for the 6-month period between October 2023 and March 2024. The schedule listed seven issuances of bonds with tenors ranging from 1 year to 20 years, and a total issuance size of HKD14 billion. The monetary authority noted that the schedule and issuance details may be adjusted based on market conditions.

## Indonesia

### Bank Indonesia Commences Sale of New Monetary Operation Instrument

On 15 September, Bank Indonesia held its first auction of Bank Indonesia Rupiah Securities (SRBI), a new monetary operation instrument that utilizes the central bank's holdings of government bonds as the underlying asset. The new instrument aims to deepen the money market, attract foreign capital flows, and optimize the government bond holdings of Bank Indonesia. The SRBI will be denominated in Indonesian rupiah and offered in maturities of 6 months, 9 months, and 12 months. Both domestic and foreign investors can participate in SRBI trades in the secondary market. The initial auction was well-received, attracting bids amounting to IDR29.9 trillion versus a target of IDR7.0 trillion.

### Indonesian Parliament Approves 2024 State Budget

In September, the Indonesian Parliament approved the government's proposed 2024 state budget, which projects state revenue at IDR2,802.3 trillion, while expenditures are programmed at IDR3,325.1 trillion. The 2024 budget was higher by about 6.5% compared with the 2023 budget and estimates a deficit equivalent to 2.3% of gross domestic product (GDP). Among the underlying macroeconomic assumptions for the budget include (i) GDP growth of 5.2%, (ii) an inflation rate of 2.8%, and (iii) an exchange rate of IDR15,000–USD1.

# Republic of Korea

## The Bank of Korea, Financial Services Commission, and the Financial Supervisory Service Announce Central Bank Digital Currency Pilot Project

On 4 October, the Bank of Korea, the Financial Services Commission, and the Financial Supervisory Service announced the Central Bank Digital Currency (CBDC) pilot project for the development of a future monetary system. The Bank for International Settlements provided technical advice. The project is intended to assess the possibility of a future monetary system where commercial banks will utilize a wholesale CBDC for interbank fund transfers and final settlements among financial institutions. This will be done via the issuance of payment instruments in the form of tokenized deposits that will be available to the general public and circulated within the CBDC network established by the Bank of Korea.

# Malaysia

## Government of Malaysia Reduces Fiscal Deficit

On 13 October, the Government of Malaysia unveiled its fiscal policies in its budget for 2024. The budget projects the 2024 fiscal deficit to be 4.3% of Malaysia's GDP, which is lower than the projected 5.0% for 2023. This is in line with one of the objectives of the Public Finance and Fiscal Responsibility Act, which was passed on 11 October to limit the economy's fiscal deficit to 3.0% of GDP and the debt-to-GDP ratio to 60% in 3–5 years. Malaysia's Ministry of Finance projections put the debt-to-GDP ratio at 62% in 2023.

# Philippines

## Bureau of the Treasury Issues Its Second Onshore Retail Dollar Bond

On 11 October, the Bureau of the Treasury issued its second Retail Dollar Bond with a tenor of 5.5 years and a 5.75% coupon rate. Through this offering, the government raised a total of USD1.3 billion, of which USD611.2 million was awarded at the rate-setting auction on 27 September and an additional USD650.7 million was raised during the 10-day offer period. The proceeds of the bond will be used to fund the government's key expenditures as approved by the 2023 National Budget. The Philippines' last issuance of a USD-denominated Retail Treasury Bond was in September 2021 when it raised almost USD1.6 billion.

# Singapore

## Monetary Authority of Singapore Changes Schedule of Monetary Policy Statements

On 13 October, the Monetary Authority of Singapore announced that it will be releasing four regular monetary policy statements starting in 2024, two more than the usual statements currently released. The statements will be released in January, April, July, and October. This change is meant to improve the central bank's communications about its policy decisions. Even though the statements will be released quarterly, the central bank's decisions will continue to be based on the medium-term outlook of Singapore's economy to maintain low and steady consumer price inflation.

# Thailand

## Government of Thailand Announces Larger Fiscal Budget and Borrowing Plan for 2024

On 13 September, Thailand's new cabinet approved a plan for a budget of THB3.48 trillion for fiscal year 2024, up 9.0% from the previous fiscal year's budget of THB3.19 trillion. The higher budget is intended to accommodate the new government's stimulus programs, which include a digital cash handout worth THB500 billion, to boost economic growth. The government also announced that it would borrow about THB2.4 trillion for fiscal year 2024, which is 9.0% higher than the previous fiscal year's borrowing plan. The government plans to issue bonds worth THB1.25 trillion for fiscal year 2024.

# Viet Nam

## State Bank of Vietnam Issues New Circular on Foreign Borrowing Not Guaranteed by the Government

Effective 15 August, Circular No. 8 replaced the existing circular (Circular No. 12), which set out conditions for nongovernment-guaranteed foreign borrowings. The new circular limits the permitted use of foreign loans and international bonds issued by Vietnamese enterprises. Under the new circular, short-term foreign borrowings can only be used for payment and restructuring the borrower's own short-term and foreign debts, while medium- or long-term foreign borrowings can only be used for the borrower's own business plans and projects. In addition, Circular No. 8 requires the borrower to submit a detailed usage plan or debt restructuring plan that justifies the purpose of foreign borrowings to the central bank for review and loan registration process. Circular No. 8 may potentially help in preventing bond defaults by allowing short-term borrowings to serve as bridge loans in refinancing scenarios.

# How Does Inflation in Advanced Economies Affect Emerging Market Bond Yields?

Increasing oil and food prices and persistent supply chain disruptions in the post-pandemic era have contributed to elevated inflation in advanced economies, reaching highs in 2022 that had not been seen for decades.[6] Inflation in developing Asian economies has also picked up, albeit at a relatively milder pace compared to major advanced economies (**Figure 19**). Existing literature finds that inflation plays a significant role in the term structure of domestic bond yields. Higher inflation can push up domestic bond yields through higher interest rates when the central bank tightens its monetary stance to ease inflationary pressure and market expectations of higher future inflation. In the international context, higher bond yields in advanced markets could also spillover to emerging market bond markets via bond market comovements and monetary policy tightening in emerging markets that follows advanced economies. Yet, there is limited evidence on how advanced economies' inflation transmits to emerging market bond yields in terms of a time series framework.

After major advanced economies and most regional economies aggressively hiked interest rates in 2022, interest rates have remained high and inflation in major advanced economies has stayed well above policy targets. Thus, it is very timely to understand how inflation in major advanced economies can impact emerging East Asian bond markets. Assessing this relationship under current market conditions has important implications for policy makers and participants in emerging East Asian bond markets.

This study examines two distinct channels that transmit advanced economy inflation to emerging market bond yields by employing a novel multivariable smooth transition autoregressive–vector autoregressive (STAR-VAR) model. To do so, we investigate the following two research questions. First, we ask whether advanced economies' inflation is linked to emerging market bond yields; second, we seek to understand how such impacts are transmitted under different market conditions. In particular, we investigate the different impacts of advanced economy inflation on emerging market bond yields during expansionary versus contractionary regimes, which feature rising and declining interest rates, respectively. The findings will have important implications under current market conditions in which inflation in advanced economies remains persistent and interest rates in emerging markets are at relatively high levels following aggressive rate hikes by regional central banks in 2021.

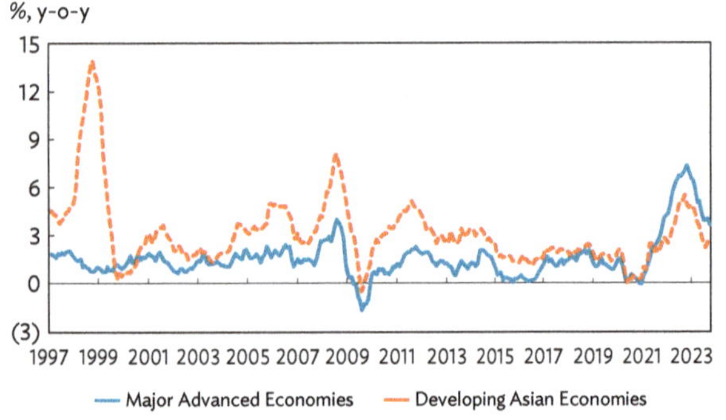

**Figure 19: Average Inflation in Major Advanced Economies and Average Inflation in Developing Asian Economies**



y-o-y = year-on-year.
Notes:
1. The solid line represents the average inflation rate of the euro area, Japan, and the United States. The dotted line represents the average inflation rate of the People's Republic of China; Hong Kong China; Indonesia; the Republic of Korea; Malaysia; the Philippines; Singapore; and Thailand.
2. Data cover the period January 1997 to September 2023.

Sources: Bloomberg LP and Haver Analytics.

---


[6] This special section was written by Sei-Wan Kim (swan@ewha.ac.kr), Department of Economics, Ewha Women's University, Seoul, Republic of Korea; Donghyun Park (dpark@adb.org), Asian Development Bank (ADB), Manila, Philippines; and Shu Tian (stian@adb.org), ADB, Manila, Philippines. The findings and analysis are based on ADB. 2023. "How Does Inflation in Advanced Economies Affect Emerging Market Bond Yields? Empirical Evidence from Two Channels." ADB Economics Working Paper 695.

Our empirical analysis yields two new key findings. First, advanced economy inflation has a significant effect on regime changes between expansion and contraction in emerging market bond yields. Second, the short-run effect of advanced economy inflation on the bond yields of emerging markets is asymmetric between the expansion and contraction regimes. The effect is mostly positive in both regimes but stronger in a bond yield's contraction regime. This suggests that the response of emerging market bond yields to advanced economy inflation does not necessarily follow a simple Fisher equation relationship.[7] We further find that advanced economy inflation triggers regime changes in emerging markets bond yields in the long run.

**Figure 20** illustrates the impacts of inflation in three advanced economies—the United States (US), Japan, and Germany—on Indonesia's bond yields with maturities of 1 year, 3 years, 5 years, and 10 years by employing a simple linear vector autoregressive model.[8] The cumulative net effects are visualized using arrows, where thicker arrows indicate stronger cumulative net effects. As shown, inflation from the three major advanced economies all have positive impacts on Indonesia's bond

yields. US inflation has a larger cumulative net effect on Indonesia's short-term bond yields (1 year and 3 years) than long-term bond yields (5 years and 10 years). Compared to the US, Germany's and Japan's inflation have relatively smaller impacts on Indonesia's 1-year and 3-year bond yields, but larger impacts on Indonesia's 10-year bond yields.

**Figure 21** further illustrates these impacts by employing a STAR-VAR model, which provides more information on how advanced economies' inflation affects bond yields in emerging markets asymmetrically during expansion and contraction regimes. In Figure 21, the upper part demonstrates impacts during the contractionary regime of bond yields, while the lower part depicts the impacts during the expansionary regime. Thicker arrows indicate stronger cumulative net effects. As shown, advanced economies' inflation has different impacts on Indonesia's bond yields during contraction and expansion regimes. First, inflation in advanced economies positively affects Indonesia's bond yields during contraction regimes (the upper part of the Figure 21). In particular, both the US' and Germany's inflation demonstrate larger impacts on long-term bond yields (5 years and 10 years) compared

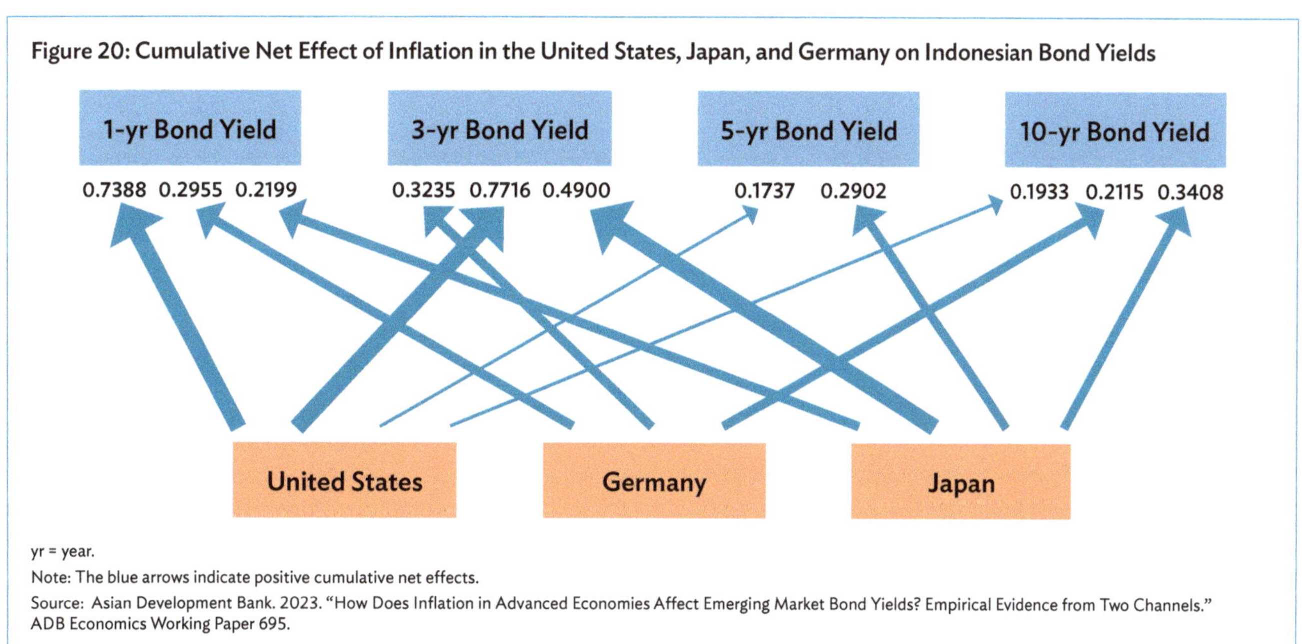

Figure 20: Cumulative Net Effect of Inflation in the United States, Japan, and Germany on Indonesian Bond Yields



yr = year.

Note: The blue arrows indicate positive cumulative net effects.

Source: Asian Development Bank. 2023. "How Does Inflation in Advanced Economies Affect Emerging Market Bond Yields? Empirical Evidence from Two Channels." ADB Economics Working Paper 695.

---

[7]  The simple Fisher equation relationship expresses the one-to-one relationship between nominal interest rates and inflation. Mathematically it can be expressed as the nominal interest rate being the sum of the real interest rate and inflation.

[8]  The same empirical analysis was implemented for other emerging East Asian markets, including the People's Republic of China; Hong Kong, China; the Republic of Korea; Malaysia; the Philippines; and Thailand. Market-specific evidence can be found in Asian Development Bank. 2023. "How Does Inflation in Advanced Economies Affect Emerging Market Bond Yields? Empirical Evidence from Two Channels." ADB Economics Working Paper 695.

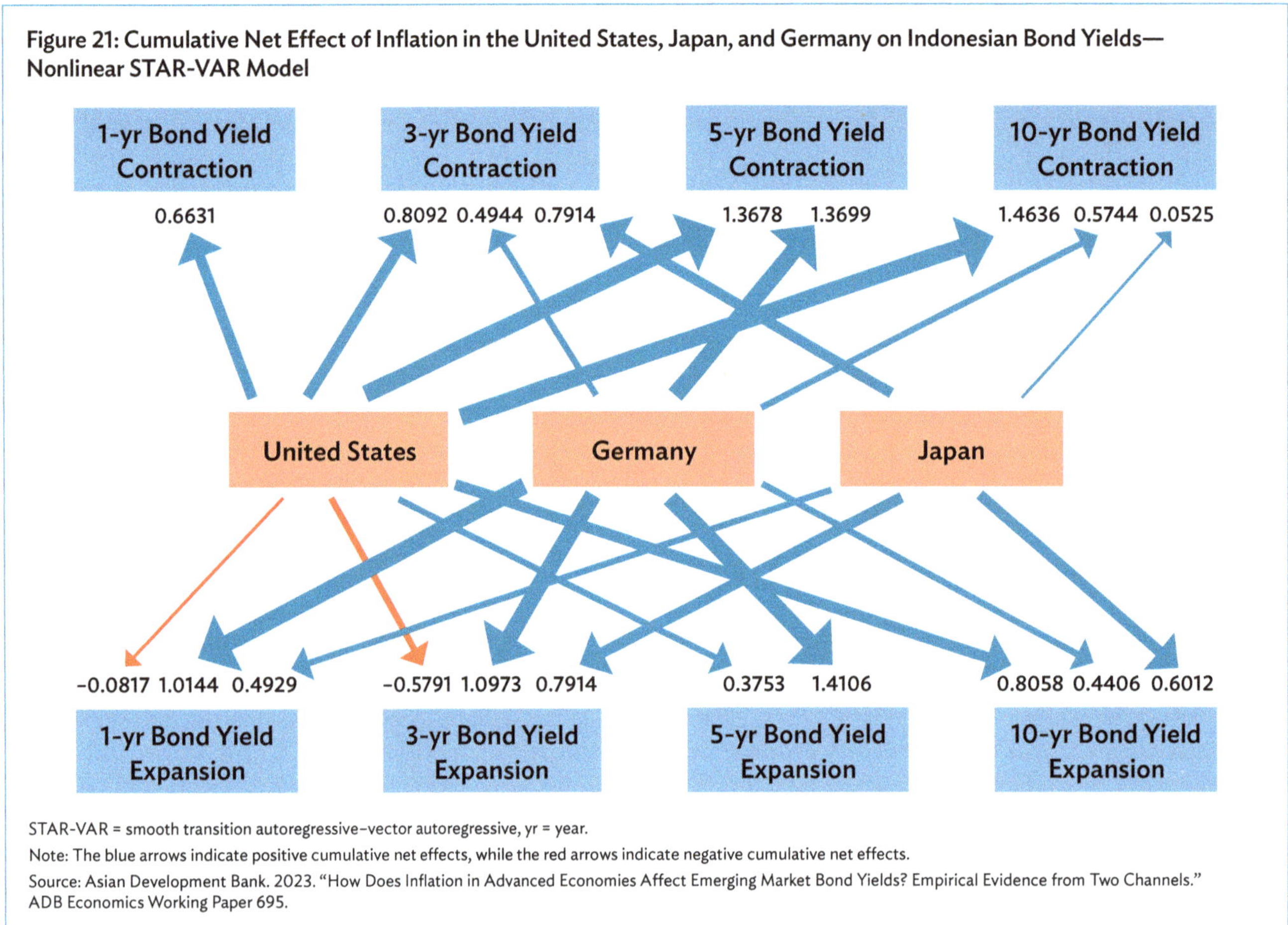

**Figure 21: Cumulative Net Effect of Inflation in the United States, Japan, and Germany on Indonesian Bond Yields—Nonlinear STAR-VAR Model**



STAR-VAR = smooth transition autoregressive–vector autoregressive, yr = year.
Note: The blue arrows indicate positive cumulative net effects, while the red arrows indicate negative cumulative net effects.
Source: Asian Development Bank. 2023. "How Does Inflation in Advanced Economies Affect Emerging Market Bond Yields? Empirical Evidence from Two Channels." ADB Economics Working Paper 695.

to short-term bond yields (1 year and 3 years) during a bond yield contraction period. Japan's inflation has a relatively larger impact on 3-year bond yields during the same period. Second, during a bond yield expansion regime, US inflation only positively affects long-term bond yields (5 years and 10 years), and its impact switches to negative for short-term bond yields (1 year and 3 years), as represented by red arrows in the lower part of graph. Meanwhile, Japan's and Germany's inflation both have positive impacts on Indonesian bond yields for all maturities, with relatively larger impacts for 3-year and 5-year bond yields, respectively. In sum, STAR-VAR model estimation reveals the presence of asymmetric impacts of advanced economies' inflation on short-term bond yields in Indonesia. Moreover, during an expansion regime, US inflation has a larger impact on Indonesia's long-term interest rates (10-year bond yields) than either Germany's or Japan's.

Evidence from other emerging East Asian markets shows positive impacts from inflation in advanced economies on bond yields under both contractionary and expansionary bond market regimes. However, the effect is relatively weak or inelastic under an expansionary regime, but stronger or more elastic under a contractionary regime in most cases. More importantly, there is evidence that inflation in advanced economies triggers switches in emerging market bond yield regimes. This suggests that the response of emerging market bond yields to advanced economy inflation does not necessarily follow a simple Fisher equation relationship; the Fisher relationship becomes more regime dependent. Since the intensity of the positive effects of advanced economy inflation changes between contractionary and expansionary regimes, we refer to the effects as "dynamic Fisher effects."

# Market Summaries

## People's Republic of China

### Yield Movements

**Between the review period of 1 September and 10 November, local currency (LCY) government bond yields in the People's Republic of China (PRC) rose for most maturities following cues from the United States Federal Reserve that it would leave policy rates elevated for an extended period (Figure 1).** Yields rose more at the shorter-end, with the 2-year yield rising 22 basis points while the 10-year yield rose only 2 basis points, capped by nonexistent inflation of 0.0% year-on-year (y-o-y) from 0.1% y-o-y in September, as well as a decline in gross domestic product growth from 6.3% y-o-y in the second quarter of 2023 to 4.9% y-o-y in the third quarter (Q3), which was still higher than expected. Also dragging on the economic outlook were continued property market woes. Country Garden declared a default on 25 October, triggering a payout of its credit default swaps. Evergrande is also still in ongoing talks regarding the restructuring of its debt.

### Local Currency Bond Market Size and Issuance

**LCY bonds outstanding in the PRC posted a modest expansion in Q3 2023 as the government urged local governments to complete their bond quotas by September 2023 (Figure 2).** Overall LCY bonds outstanding in the PRC rose 2.5% quarter-on-quarter (q-o-q) to CNY136.3 trillion at the end of September. By sector, government bonds outstanding grew 3.3% q-o-q to CNY90.8 trillion as local governments sought to completely utilize their bond quota by the end of September. Corporate bonds outstanding grew 1.1% q-o-q to CNY45.5 trillion.

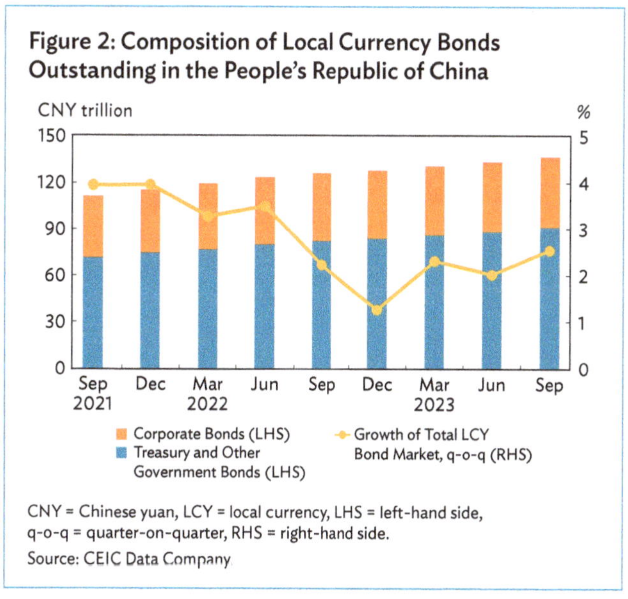

Figure 2: Composition of Local Currency Bonds Outstanding in the People's Republic of China



CNY = Chinese yuan, LCY = local currency, LHS = left-hand side, q-o-q = quarter-on-quarter, RHS = right-hand side.
Source: CEIC Data Company.

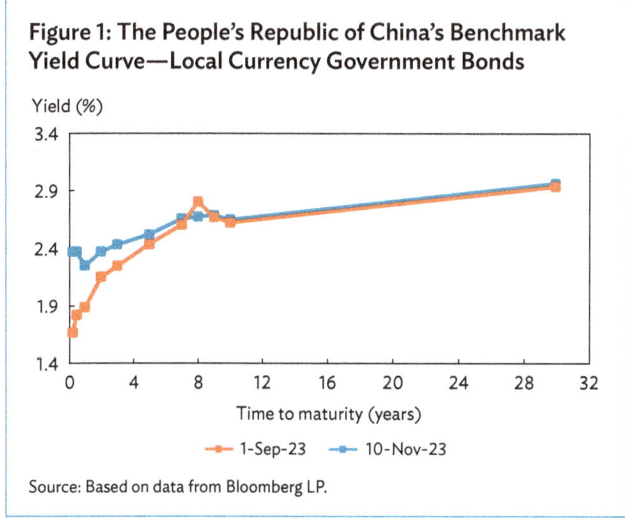

Figure 1: The People's Republic of China's Benchmark Yield Curve—Local Currency Government Bonds



Source: Based on data from Bloomberg LP.

**LCY bond sales in the PRC totaled CNY12.0 trillion in Q3 2023, growing 11.5% q-o-q largely due to local government bond issuance (Figure 3).** Issuance of Treasury and other government bonds climbed 15.5% q-o-q in Q3 2023 to CNY7.0 trillion. Corporate bond issuance growth moderated to 6.5% q-o-q to CNY5.0 trillion from 11.8% q-o-q in the second quarter as bond defaults weighed on investor sentiment.

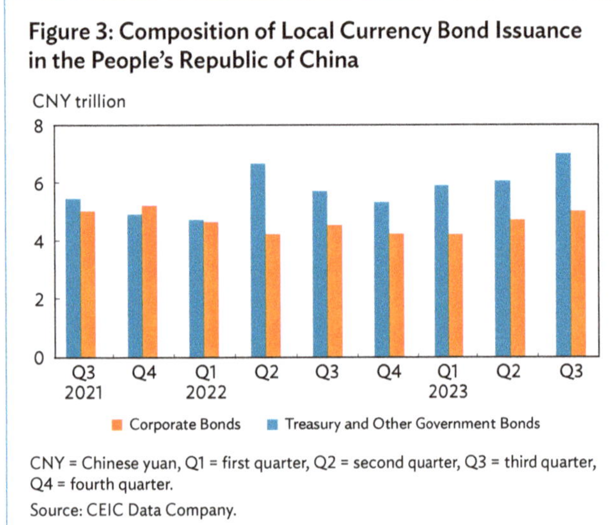

**Figure 3: Composition of Local Currency Bond Issuance in the People's Republic of China**



CNY = Chinese yuan, Q1 = first quarter, Q2 = second quarter, Q3 = third quarter, Q4 = fourth quarter.
Source: CEIC Data Company.

## Investor Profile

**Commercial banks remained the largest holder of government bonds at the end of September (Figure 4).** Commercial banks are the dominant investor in the PRC with such a high share that the PRC has the second-highest Herfindahl–Hirschman Index score in emerging East Asia.[9] Commercial banks held nearly 80% of total government bonds outstanding at the end of September and were the most active in local government bond purchases with a share of 85.4%.

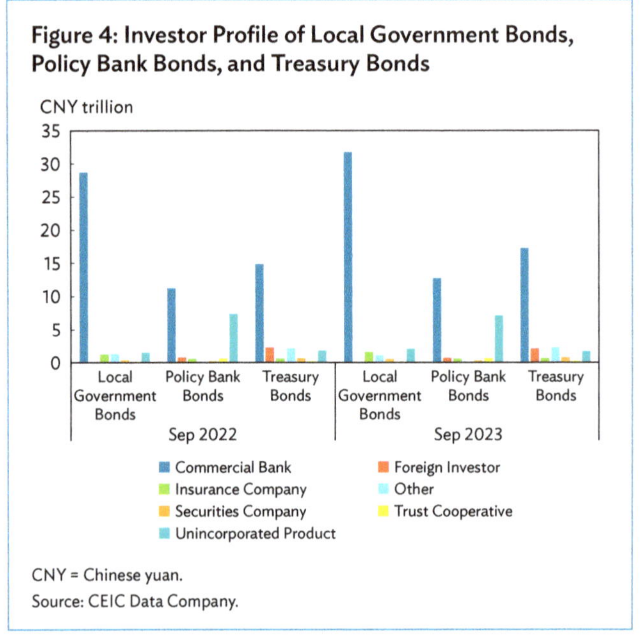

**Figure 4: Investor Profile of Local Government Bonds, Policy Bank Bonds, and Treasury Bonds**



CNY = Chinese yuan.
Source: CEIC Data Company.

---

[9] The Herfindahl–Hirschman Index is a commonly accepted measure of market concentration. In this case, the index was used to measure the investor profile diversification of the local currency bond market and is calculated by summing the squared share of each investor group in the bond market.

# Hong Kong, China

## Yield Movements

**Between 1 September and 10 November, local currency (LCY) government bond yields in Hong Kong, China rose across all tenors (Figure 1).** The average yield increase was 70 basis points, with more pronounced increases for short-term bonds. The rise in yields was primarily driven by expectations that the United States Federal Reserve will maintain higher interest rates longer than previously expected as well as growing uncertainty stemming from the impacts on the domestic economy of a global economic slowdown and geopolitical tensions.

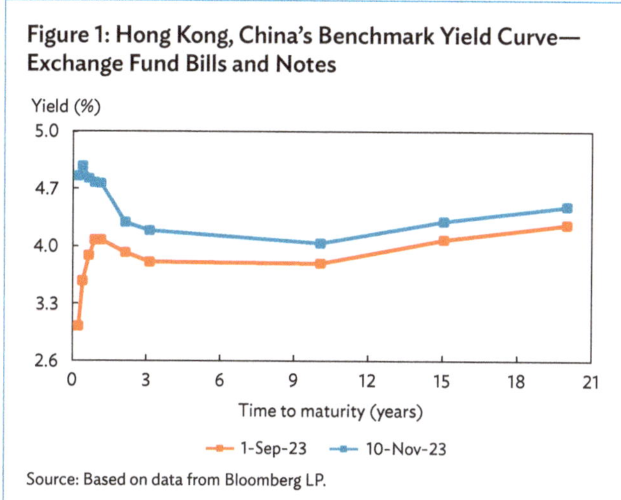

Figure 1: Hong Kong, China's Benchmark Yield Curve—Exchange Fund Bills and Notes



Source: Based on data from Bloomberg LP.

## Local Currency Bond Market Size and Issuance

**LCY bonds outstanding in Hong Kong, China expanded to HKD3.0 trillion at the end of September, posting 5.1% quarter-on-quarter (q-o-q) growth.** This was driven by the increase in both government and corporate outstanding bonds (**Figure 2**). Hong Kong Special Administrative Region (HKSAR) bonds outstanding reached HKD0.3 trillion, growing by 23.2% q-o-q due to a large issuance of retail government bonds in the third quarter (Q3) of 2023. Meanwhile, the LCY corporate bonds outstanding rose 5.6% q-o-q to reach HKD1.5 trillion, and they maintained a share of nearly half of Hong Kong, China's total LCY bond market. Exchange Fund Bills and Exchange Fund Notes (HKD1.2 trillion) comprised 41.1% of total outstanding LCY bonds at the end of September, while HKSAR bonds accounted for the remaining 9.6% share.

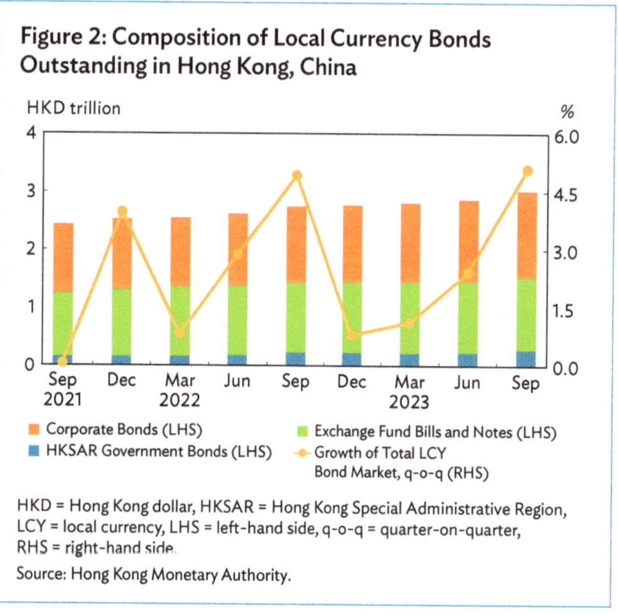

Figure 2: Composition of Local Currency Bonds Outstanding in Hong Kong, China



HKD = Hong Kong dollar, HKSAR = Hong Kong Special Administrative Region, LCY = local currency, LHS = left-hand side, q-o-q = quarter-on-quarter, RHS = right-hand side.

Source: Hong Kong Monetary Authority.

**LCY bond issuance in Hong Kong, China picked up in Q3 2023 due largely to a rebound in corporate bond sales** (**Figure 3**). Total bond issuance registered HKD1.3 trillion in Q3 2023, up 7.8% from the previous quarter. Corporate debt sales recovered, rising 22.9% q-o-q to HKD263.3 billion due to improved investor sentiment amid sustained economic growth. Hong Kong Mortgage Corporation was the top nonbank corporate issuer during the quarter with total issuance amounting to HKD14.7 billion. Meanwhile, HKSAR bond issuance jumped to HKD58.5 billion in Q3 2023 from HKD9.5 billion in the previous quarter, driven primarily by a HKD55.0 billion Silver Bond issuance in August.[10] Issuance of Exchange Fund Bills and Exchange Fund Notes totaled HKD994.6 billion in Q3 2023, down 0.3% from the previous quarter.

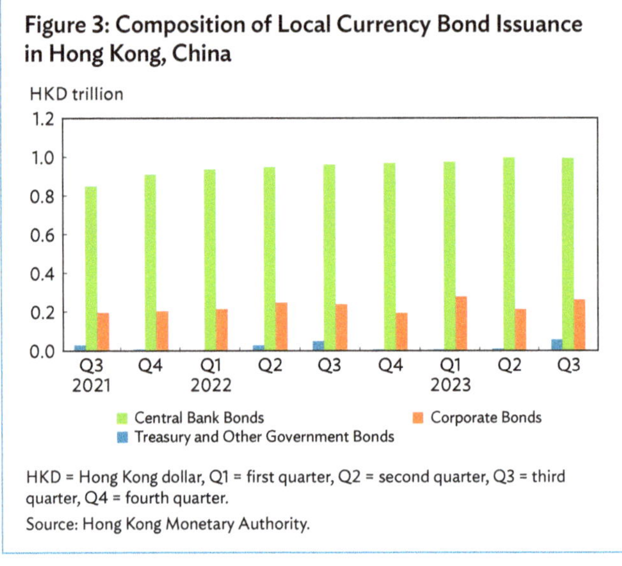

**Figure 3: Composition of Local Currency Bond Issuance in Hong Kong, China**



HKD = Hong Kong dollar, Q1 = first quarter, Q2 = second quarter, Q3 = third quarter, Q4 = fourth quarter.
Source: Hong Kong Monetary Authority.

---

[10]  Silver Bonds are 3-year inflation-linked government bonds intended for purchase by citizens 60 years and older.

# Indonesia

## Yield Movements

**Local currency (LCY) government bond yields in Indonesia rose for all maturities from 1 September to 10 November** (**Figure 1**). Yields climbed an average of 48 basis points across the curve, largely driven by the United States Federal Reserve hinting that it would keep rates elevated for an extended period and the unexpected rate hike by Bank Indonesia on its 18–19 October Board of Governors meeting. Bank Indonesia raised the 7-day reverse repurchase rate by 25 basis points to support rupiah stability and avert further capital outflows from its financial market. In addition, the government programmed a higher bond issuance target in the fourth quarter of 2023 to support increased government spending in the latter part of the year.

## Local Currency Bond Market Size and Issuance

**LCY bond market growth in Indonesia rebounded in the third quarter (Q3) of 2023, buoyed by increased issuance of government bonds during the quarter.** The LCY bond market posted growth of 0.5% quarter-on-quarter (q-o-q), after a 0.5% q-o-q contraction in the second quarter, with the market's size reaching IDR6,163.4 trillion at the end of September (**Figure 2**). Growth was largely generated by an increase in the stock of outstanding government bonds due to higher issuance volume in Q3 2023. On the other hand, the outstanding stock of corporate bonds posted a marginal decline as the volume of issuance was more than offset by maturities during the quarter.

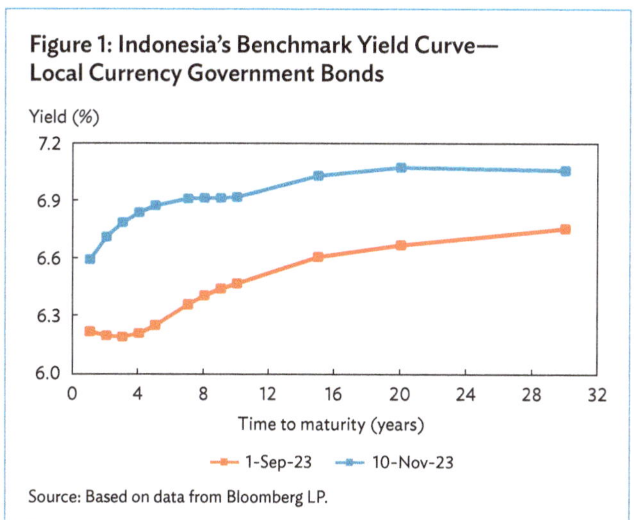

**Figure 1: Indonesia's Benchmark Yield Curve—Local Currency Government Bonds**



Source: Based on data from Bloomberg LP.

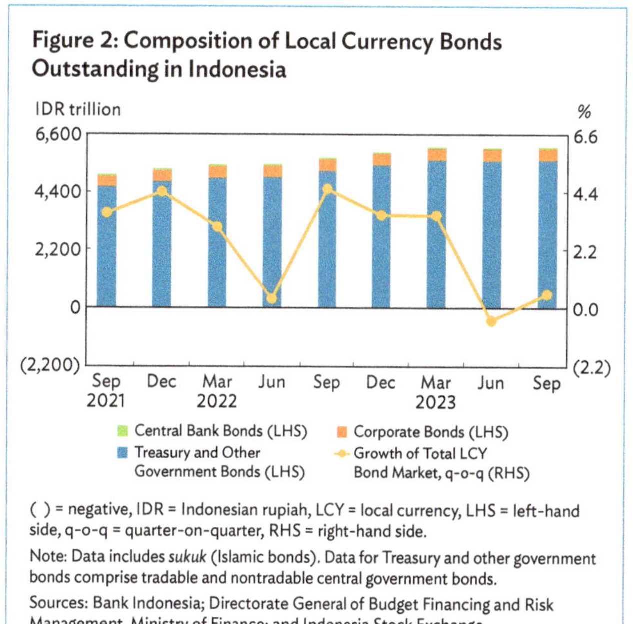

**Figure 2: Composition of Local Currency Bonds Outstanding in Indonesia**



( ) = negative, IDR = Indonesian rupiah, LCY = local currency, LHS = left-hand side, q-o-q = quarter-on-quarter, RHS = right-hand side.

Note: Data includes *sukuk* (Islamic bonds). Data for Treasury and other government bonds comprise tradable and nontradable central government bonds.

Sources: Bank Indonesia; Directorate General of Budget Financing and Risk Management, Ministry of Finance; and Indonesia Stock Exchange.

**LCY bond issuance in Indonesia tallied IDR406.0 trillion in Q3 2023 on growth of 16.1% q-o-q amid still elevated interest rates (Figure 3).** Treasury bond issuance rose 27.9% q-o-q following tepid issuance in the previous quarter. However, some Treasury auctions during the quarter were not fully awarded as investors sought higher rates. Corporate bond issuance also grew more than two-fold during the quarter. The largest corporate bond issuances during the quarter came from Indah Kiat Pulp & Paper, Bank Mandiri, and Lontar Papyrus, which accounted for 14.9%, 11.6%, and 6.9%, respectively, of the Q3 2023 corporate issuance total.

## Investor Profile

**Domestic investors remained the largest holder of tradable central government bonds in Indonesia.** By the end of September, local investor holdings comprised 82.4% of conventional bonds and an even larger share of 98.2% for Islamic bonds (**Figure 4**). Overall, banking institutions were the largest holders of government bonds, accounting for about a third of the total tradable bonds at the end of September. All other investor groups accounted for an average holdings share of 16.7%, except for mutual funds (3.3%). Among regional peers, Indonesia had the most diverse investor holdings, as measured by its score on the Herfindahl–Hirschman Index.[11]

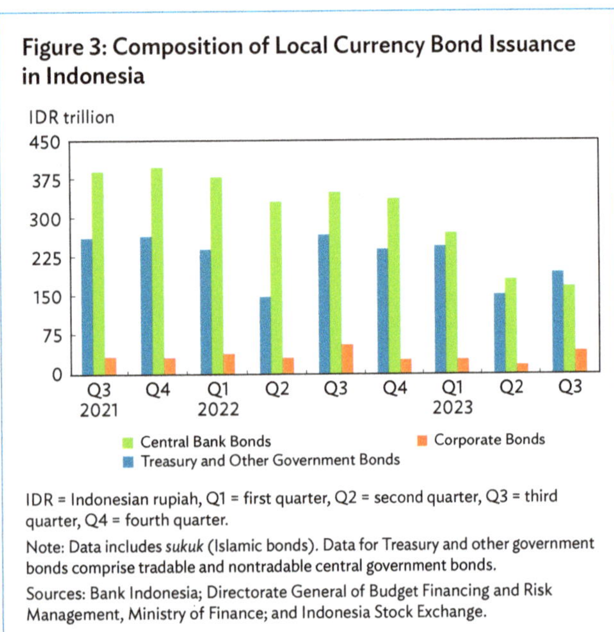

**Figure 3: Composition of Local Currency Bond Issuance in Indonesia**



IDR = Indonesian rupiah, Q1 = first quarter, Q2 = second quarter, Q3 = third quarter, Q4 = fourth quarter.

Note: Data includes *sukuk* (Islamic bonds). Data for Treasury and other government bonds comprise tradable and nontradable central government bonds.

Sources: Bank Indonesia; Directorate General of Budget Financing and Risk Management, Ministry of Finance; and Indonesia Stock Exchange.

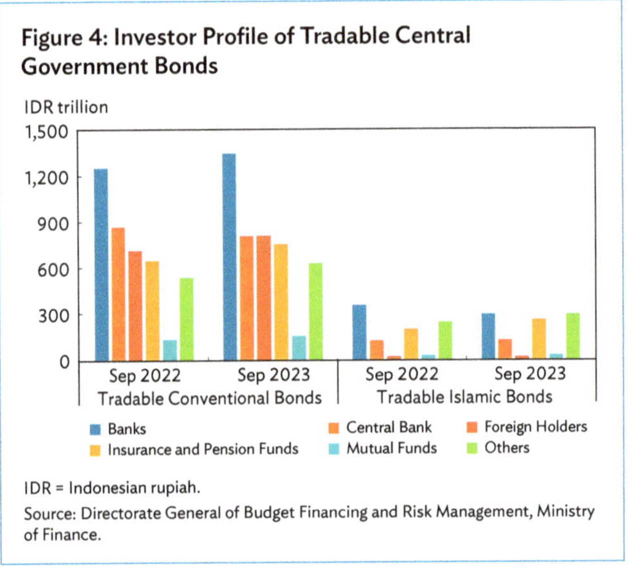

**Figure 4: Investor Profile of Tradable Central Government Bonds**



IDR = Indonesian rupiah.

Source: Directorate General of Budget Financing and Risk Management, Ministry of Finance.

---

[11] The Herfindahl–Hirschman Index is a common measure of market concentration. The index was used to measure the investor profile diversification of the local currency bond market and is calculated by summing the squared share of each investor group in the bond market.

# Republic of Korea

## Yield Movements

Local currency (LCY) government bond yields in the Republic of Korea rose for most tenors between 1 September and 10 November on expectations of a prolonged tight monetary stance from the United States Federal Reserve (**Figure 1**). The Bank of Korea (BOK) at its 19 October monetary policy meeting kept the base rate at 3.50% amid higher inflation and growth uncertainties due to the Federal Reserve's signal of an extended period of elevated rates, rising household debt in the domestic market, and recent geopolitical tensions. These factors pushed up the yields during the review period. Market expectations of the BOK's continued restrictive monetary policy for the rest of the year also pushed up yields. The BOK stated that although inflation is expected to slow, it may remain above 3.0% for the remainder of the year, which is still higher than the 2.0% target.

## Local Currency Bond Market Size and Issuance

LCY bonds outstanding in the Republic of Korea rose 2.4% quarter-on-quarter (q-o-q) to KRW3,166.8 trillion at the end of the third quarter (Q3) of 2023, driven by growth in both the government and corporate bond segments. Corporate bonds continued to comprise more than half of total bonds outstanding in Q3 2023 and posted growth of 3.3% q-o-q, while government bonds outstanding rose at a slower pace of 1.2% q-o-q in Q3 2023 (**Figure 2**). Overall growth in Q3 2023 moderated from 2.6% q-o-q in the previous quarter due to a decline in quarterly issuances across all types of bonds.

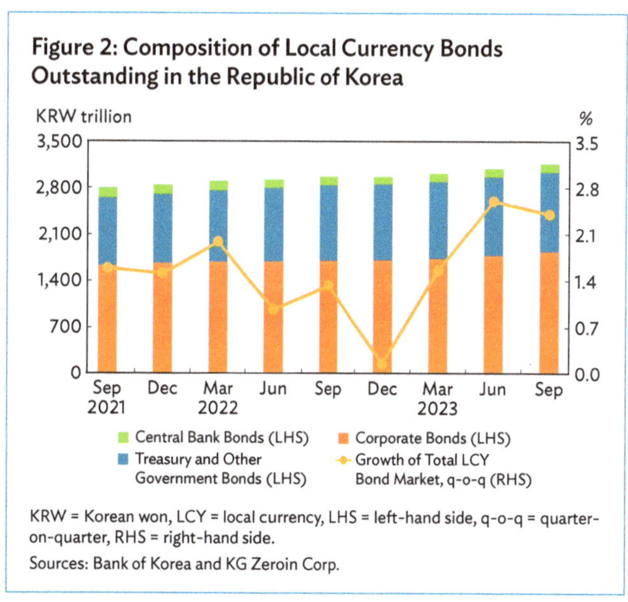

**Figure 2: Composition of Local Currency Bonds Outstanding in the Republic of Korea**



KRW = Korean won, LCY = local currency, LHS = left-hand side, q-o-q = quarter-on-quarter, RHS = right-hand side.
Sources: Bank of Korea and KG Zeroin Corp.

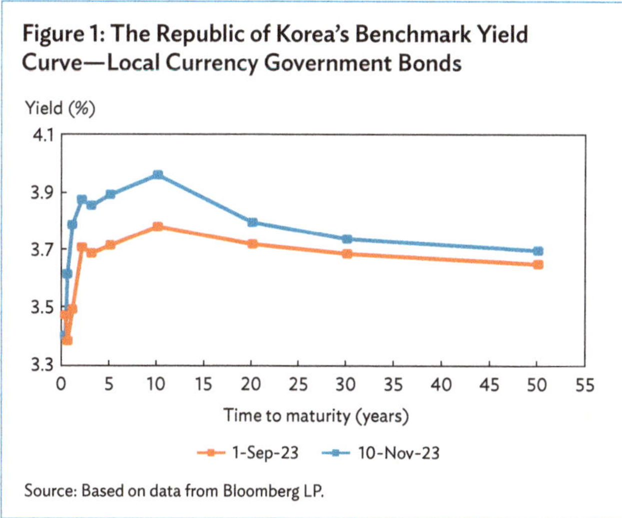

**Figure 1: The Republic of Korea's Benchmark Yield Curve—Local Currency Government Bonds**



Source: Based on data from Bloomberg LP.

**Total LCY bond issuance fell 7.2% q-o-q to KRW290.2 trillion in Q3 2023 as issuance declined for all bond segments.** Government bonds issuance in Q3 2023 declined 12.9% q-o-q from a relatively high base in the second quarter of 2023 as the government had pursued a frontloading policy of releasing 65% of the 2023 budget in the first half of the year (**Figure 3**). Issuance of corporate bonds also fell, but at a slower pace of 3.8% q-o-q, due to higher borrowing costs amid a prolonged high-interest-rate environment. Corporate bond issuance in Q3 2023 continued to be dominated by banks and financial institutions.

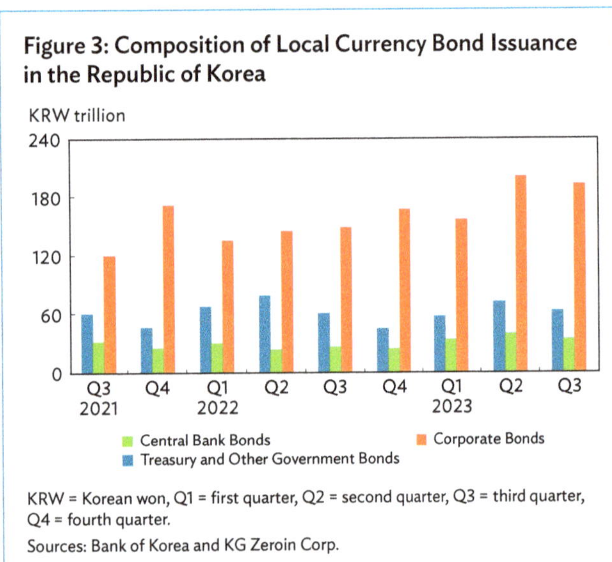

**Figure 3: Composition of Local Currency Bond Issuance in the Republic of Korea**



KRW = Korean won, Q1 = first quarter, Q2 = second quarter, Q3 = third quarter, Q4 = fourth quarter.
Sources: Bank of Korea and KG Zeroin Corp.

## Investor Profile

**Insurance companies and pension funds remained the largest investor group in the Republic of Korea's LCY bond market at the end of June 2023.** They held a collective 28.4% share of the LCY bond market, but this was lower than their 32.3% share from a year ago. Insurance companies and pension funds accounted for more than 25% of all holdings in both the government and corporate bond markets (**Figure 4**). However, other financial institutions collectively had the largest holdings share in the corporate bond market at the end of June with 44.6% of the total. Foreign holdings in the LCY corporate bond market remained negligible in the second quarter of 2023, but foreign holdings in the LCY government bond market increased to 20.0% at the end of June from 18.4% a year earlier. Foreign holdings of LCY government bonds may have declined in Q3 2023 as bonds registered smaller net foreign inflows in July and reversed to net outflows in August and September. Foreign investors sold domestic bonds in recent months due to the weakening of the Korean won and the widening interest rate differential with US Treasuries, whose yields rose at a more rapid pace, making returns on Korean yields less attractive.

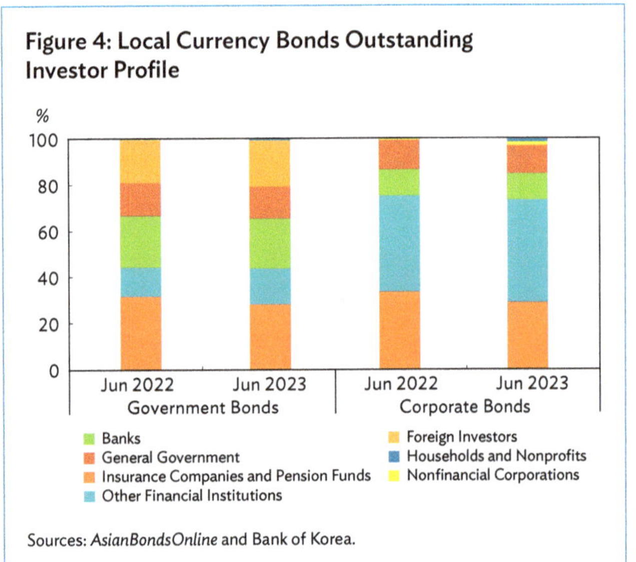

**Figure 4: Local Currency Bonds Outstanding Investor Profile**



Sources: *AsianBondsOnline* and Bank of Korea.

# Malaysia

## Yield Movements

**Malaysia's local currency (LCY) government bond yields increased between 1 September and 10 November (Figure 1).** The yield curve of Malaysia shifted upward, broadly mirroring the movement in United States Treasury yields during the review period. At its 2 November meeting, Bank Negara Malaysia kept its overnight policy rate steady at 3.00%. Investors remained cautious as the United States Federal Reserve indicated that it would keep interest rates elevated longer than previously forecast.

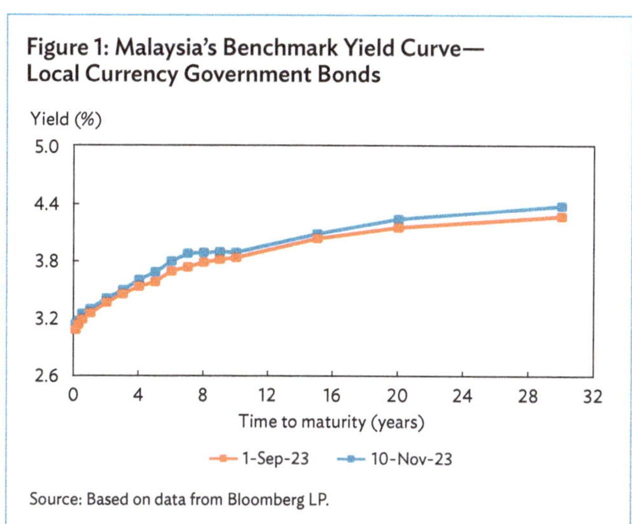

**Figure 1: Malaysia's Benchmark Yield Curve— Local Currency Government Bonds**



Source: Based on data from Bloomberg LP.

## Local Currency Bond Market Size and Issuance

**The size of Malaysia's LCY bond market increased in the third quarter (Q3) of 2023.** LCY bonds outstanding grew 1.5% quarter-on-quarter (q-o-q), reaching MYR1,982.6 billion at the end of September (**Figure 2**). All LCY bond types expanded in Q3 2023—led by Bank Negara Malaysia bills, which grew 29.2% q-o-q— as the stock of fixed-income securities increased and corporate bonds grew 1.7% q-o-q on higher supply. Government-owned finance company DanaInfra Nasional remained the top corporate bond issuer at the end of September 2023, with a total of MYR82.2 billion of outstanding corporate bonds.

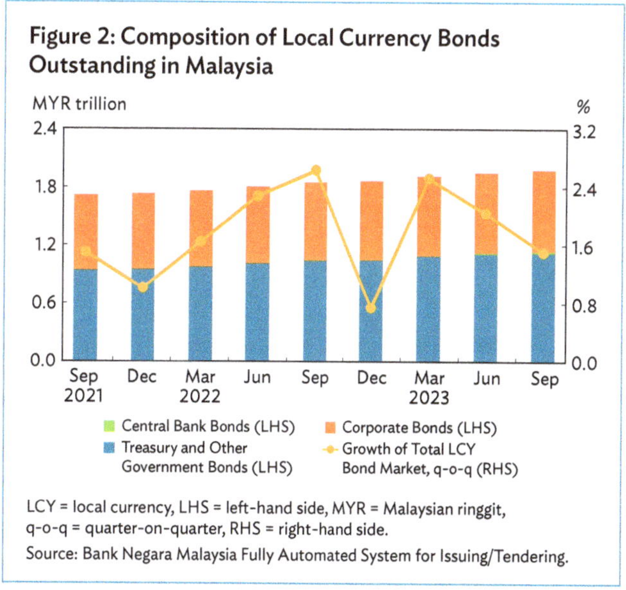

**Figure 2: Composition of Local Currency Bonds Outstanding in Malaysia**



LCY = local currency, LHS = left-hand side, MYR = Malaysian ringgit, q-o-q = quarter-on-quarter, RHS = right-hand side.
Source: Bank Negara Malaysia Fully Automated System for Issuing/Tendering.

**LCY bonds issued in Malaysia expanded during the review period.** Issuance of LCY bonds grew 53.7% q-o-q, supported by increased issuance of central bank bills and corporate bonds (**Figure 3**). The level of issuance of Malaysian Government Securities (conventional bonds) and Government Investment Issues (*sukuk,* or Islamic bonds) was the same compared with the previous quarter. Cagamas remained the top issuer with a total of MYR5.8 billion in new issuance in Q3 2023.

**Outstanding LCY *sukuk* increased to MYR1.3 trillion at the end of September on quarterly growth of 1.0%.** *Sukuk* comprised 63.8% of Malaysia's LCY bonds outstanding at the end of Q3 2023, with Treasury and corporate *sukuk* driving the expansion of the Islamic bond market.

## Investor Profile

**Domestic investors held 76.9% of total LCY government bonds at the end of the second quarter of 2023, up slightly from the 76.0% holdings in the same period in the previous year** (**Figure 4**). Financial institutions had the largest share among investors, holding 33.5% of total LCY government bonds, which was less than the 35.2% share in the same period last year. The share of social security institutions, insurance companies, and Bank Negara Malaysia increased during the review period. On the other hand, foreign investors' share declined due to the hawkish stance of the Federal Reserve, which in September signaled that it would keep interest rates elevated for an extended period.

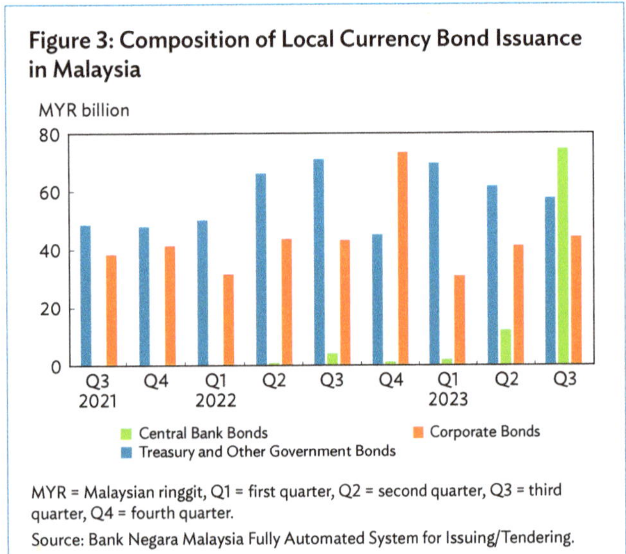

**Figure 3: Composition of Local Currency Bond Issuance in Malaysia**



MYR = Malaysian ringgit, Q1 = first quarter, Q2 = second quarter, Q3 = third quarter, Q4 = fourth quarter.
Source: Bank Negara Malaysia Fully Automated System for Issuing/Tendering.

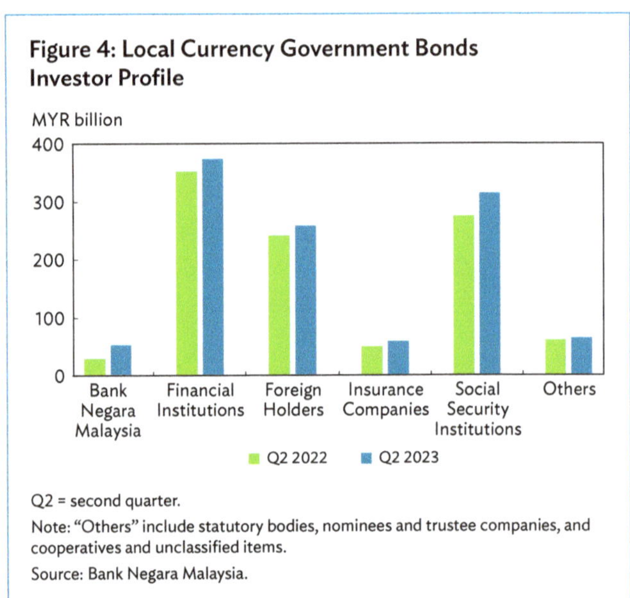

**Figure 4: Local Currency Government Bonds Investor Profile**



Q2 = second quarter.
Note: "Others" include statutory bodies, nominees and trustee companies, and cooperatives and unclassified items.
Source: Bank Negara Malaysia.

# Philippines

## Yield Movements

**Between 1 September and 10 November, local currency (LCY) government bond yields in the Philippines rose for all maturities amid persistent elevated inflation (Figure 1).** The increase in yields was driven by the Bangko Sentral ng Pilipinas' (BSP) hawkish monetary policy stance to bring inflation down within its target range of 2.0%–4.0%. Consumer price inflation accelerated in August to 5.3% year-on-year (y-o-y) from 4.7% y-o-y in July and further climbed to 6.1% y-o-y in September, driven by high food and energy prices. In an off-cycle meeting on 26 October, the BSP raised by 25 basis points the overnight reverse repurchase rate to 6.50%. The central bank is expected to keep its monetary tightening policy until inflation is brought down within the government's target even though inflation slowed to 4.9% y-o-y in October.

## Local Currency Bond Market Size and Issuance

**In the third quarter (Q3) of 2023, the Philippines' LCY bond market increased 1.8% quarter-on-quarter (q-o-q), driven by higher issuances from the government and central bank.** Outstanding central bank securities grew 44.8% q-o-q as issuance increased during the quarter to mop up excess liquidity in the market brought about by the BSP's reduction of the reserve requirement ratio and the expiration of pandemic-related relief measures on 30 June (**Figure 2**). Treasury and other government bonds outstanding posted slower growth of 0.3% q-o-q versus 2.3% q-o-q in the previous quarter, as the government failed to meet its borrowing plan for the quarter due to investors' demand for higher yields. Meanwhile, the corporate bond stock contracted 2.4% q-o-q to a size of PHP1.6 trillion, driven by reduced issuance during the quarter. Total corporate bonds outstanding were dominated by the property sector with a 31.9% share of the total LCY corporate bonds outstanding in Q3 2023.

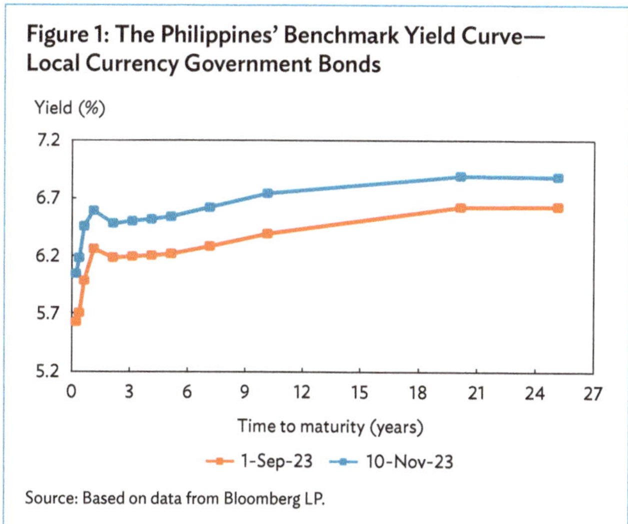

**Figure 1: The Philippines' Benchmark Yield Curve— Local Currency Government Bonds**



Source: Based on data from Bloomberg LP.

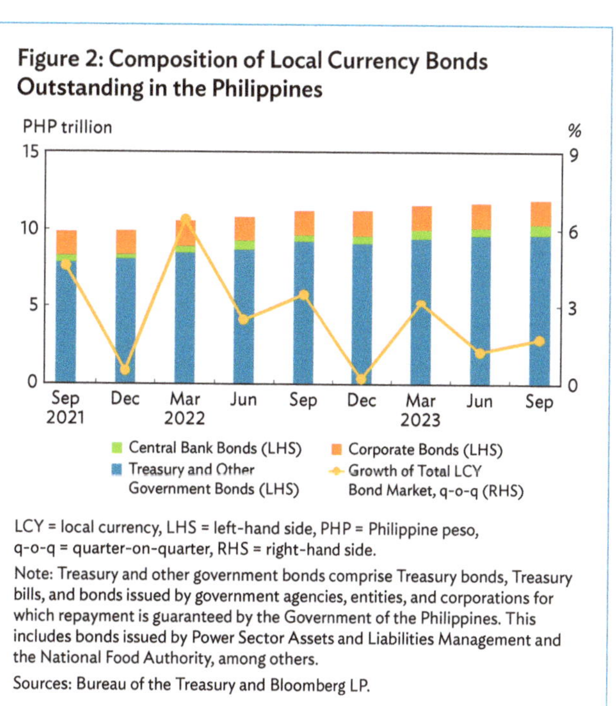

**Figure 2: Composition of Local Currency Bonds Outstanding in the Philippines**



LCY = local currency, LHS = left-hand side, PHP = Philippine peso, q-o-q = quarter-on-quarter, RHS = right-hand side.

Note: Treasury and other government bonds comprise Treasury bonds, Treasury bills, and bonds issued by government agencies, entities, and corporations for which repayment is guaranteed by the Government of the Philippines. This includes bonds issued by Power Sector Assets and Liabilities Management and the National Food Authority, among others.

Sources: Bureau of the Treasury and Bloomberg LP.

**LCY bond issuance grew 9.6% q-o-q on an expansion of government bonds and central bank securities (Figure 3).** Growth of 14.3% q-o-q in the issuance of central bank securities was buoyed by the new 56-day BSP bill that was launched on 30 June as an additional tenor under the BSP Securities Facility to effectively manage changing liquidity conditions in the economy. Issuance of Treasury and other government bonds grew 2.5% q-o-q in Q3 2023 as the government increased its borrowing plan by 25% in August from PHP180.0 billion in July due to a large volume of government bond maturities in August 2023. Meanwhile, elevated borrowing costs pushed corporate bond issuance to contract 38.8% q-o-q, or 68.5% compared to the same period in the previous year. During the quarter, only three firms tapped the bond market for funding with the largest issuance coming from Security Bank with debt sales amounting to PHP18.5 billion.

## Investor Profile

**Banks and investment houses remained the largest investor group in the economy's LCY government bond market constituting 46.6% of the total in Q3 2023 (Figure 4).** Among all other investor groups, only banks and investment houses posted an increase in their bond holdings at the end of September 2023, adding PHP400.7 billion worth of government bonds to their holdings from September 2022. Contractual savings institutions and tax-exempt institutions remained the second-largest investor group, with their holdings share dipping to 32.2% in September 2023 from 32.9% in the prior year. The holdings' share of all other investor groups stayed below 10%, while government-owned or -controlled corporations and local government units consistently held the smallest share of less than 1.0%.

**Figure 3: Composition of Local Currency Bond Issuance in the Philippines**

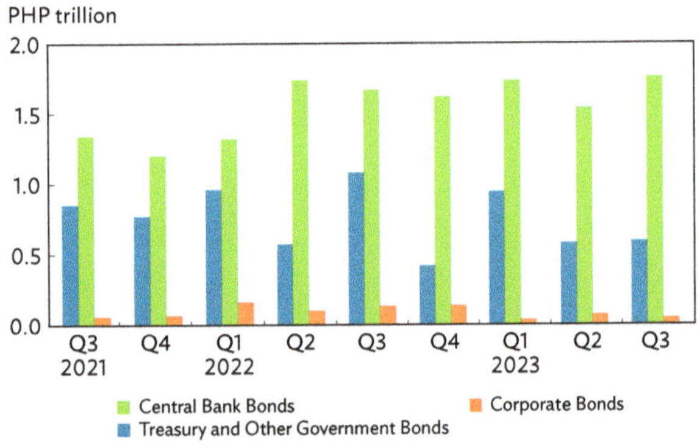

Q1 = first quarter, Q2 = second quarter, Q3 = third quarter, Q4 = fourth quarter, PHP = Philippine peso.

Note: Treasury and other government bonds comprise Treasury bonds, Treasury bills, and bonds issued by government agencies, entities, and corporations for which repayment is guaranteed by the Government of the Philippines. This includes bonds issued by Power Sector Assets and Liabilities Management and the National Food Authority, among others.

Sources: Bureau of the Treasury and Bloomberg LP.

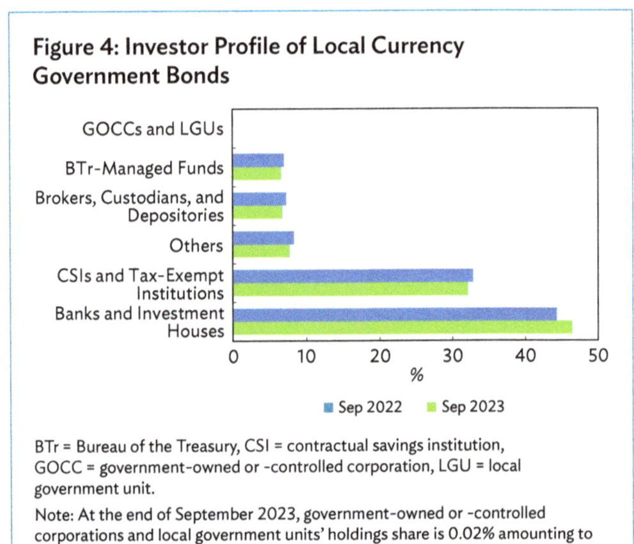

**Figure 4: Investor Profile of Local Currency Government Bonds**



BTr = Bureau of the Treasury, CSI = contractual savings institution, GOCC = government-owned or -controlled corporation, LGU = local government unit.

Note: At the end of September 2023, government-owned or -controlled corporations and local government units' holdings share is 0.02% amounting to PHP2.4 billion.

Source: Bureau of the Treasury.

# Singapore

## Yield Movements

**The local currency (LCY) government bond yields of Singapore declined for all maturities except the 6-month and 1-year yields between 1 September and 10 November (Figure 1).** Singapore was the only emerging East Asian market whose yield curve shifted downward during the review period. However, the bulk of the decline in yields came after the Federal Open Market Committee meeting on 1–2 November when the Federal Reserve hinted it may not raise rates anymore. Singapore's declining core inflation also contributed to the downward pressure on yields. The Monetary Authority of Singapore (MAS) kept the appreciation rate of its Singapore dollar nominal effective exchange rate unchanged at its October meeting.

## Local Currency Bond Market Size and Issuance

**Singapore's LCY bond market expanded in the third quarter (Q3) of 2023 (Figure 2).** Total outstanding LCY bonds increased 2.6% quarter-on-quarter (q-o-q) to SGD699.6 billion. The growth was driven by central bank securities, which increased by 4.4% q-o-q, dominating Singapore's LCY bond market as MAS securities are auctioned regularly for liquidity management purposes in the financial market. Singapore Government Securities bills and bonds expanded from the previous quarter. However, LCY corporate outstanding bonds remained subdued, contracting by 0.5% q-o-q during the review period. The Housing & Development Board remained the top corporate issuer at the end of September with a total of SGD26.8 billion of outstanding corporate bonds.

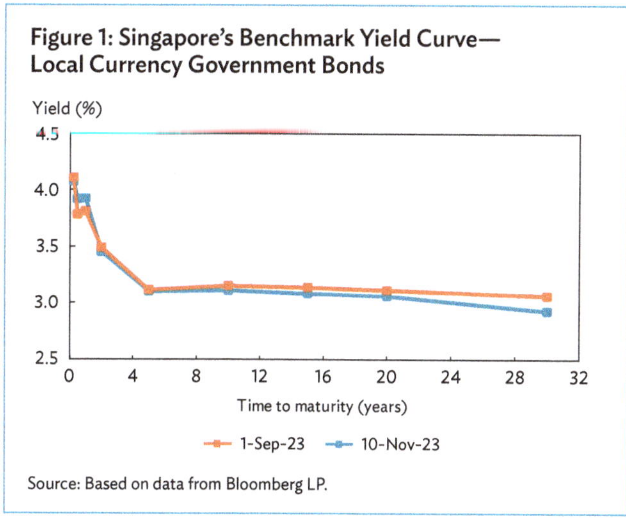

**Figure 1: Singapore's Benchmark Yield Curve— Local Currency Government Bonds**



Source: Based on data from Bloomberg LP.

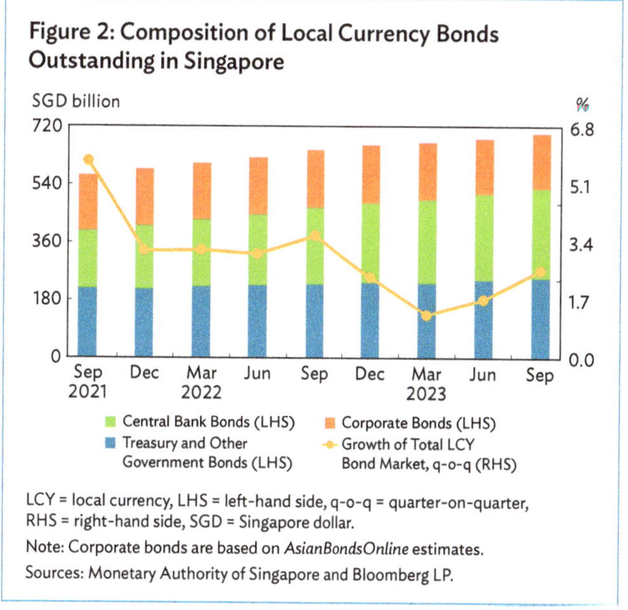

**Figure 2: Composition of Local Currency Bonds Outstanding in Singapore**



LCY = local currency, LHS = left-hand side, q-o-q = quarter-on-quarter, RHS = right-hand side, SGD = Singapore dollar.
Note: Corporate bonds are based on *AsianBondsOnline* estimates.
Sources: Monetary Authority of Singapore and Bloomberg LP.

**Total LCY bonds issued in Singapore grew in Q3 2023, albeit at a slower pace than in the previous quarter.**
Growth in LCY bond issuance decelerated to 5.4% q-o-q as the expansion in Treasury and other government bonds and central bank bills was offset by the contraction in corporate bond issuance (**Figure 3**). LCY corporate bond issuance declined by 17.3% q-o-q due to the persistently high-interest-rate environment in Singapore. Despite this, Oversea-Chinese Banking Corporation was able to raise SGD550.0 million from a perpetual callable floating-rate bond issued in August.

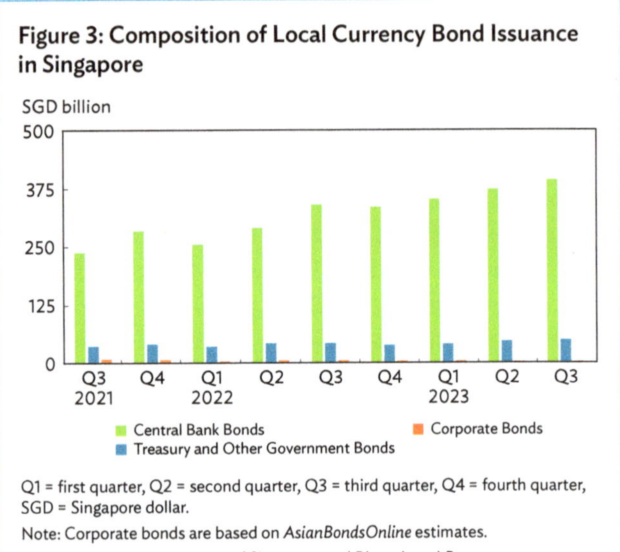

**Figure 3: Composition of Local Currency Bond Issuance in Singapore**



Q1 = first quarter, Q2 = second quarter, Q3 = third quarter, Q4 = fourth quarter, SGD = Singapore dollar.
Note: Corporate bonds are based on *AsianBondsOnline* estimates.
Sources: Monetary Authority of Singapore and Bloomberg LP.

# Thailand

## Yield Movements

**Thailand's local currency (LCY) government bond yields rose for all tenors between 1 September and 10 November (Figure 1).** This was due to the Bank of Thailand's (BOT) continued monetary policy tightening to ward off inflation. The BOT has raised its policy rate by a total of 175 basis points over seven consecutive meetings between August 2022 and August 2023. At the 27 September monetary policy meeting, the BOT again raised its benchmark rate by 25 basis points to 2.50% to guard against inflationary pressures from the new government's stimulus programs. The new administration has since announced plans to boost the economy through handouts to eligible citizens[12] totaling around THB500 billion to be distributed through digital wallets.

## Local Currency Bond Market Size and Issuance

**Thailand's LCY bond market posted steady growth in the third quarter (Q3) of 2023, reaching a size of THB16.6 trillion at the end of September.** Thailand's outstanding LCY bonds registered 1.9% quarter-on-quarter (q-o-q) growth in Q3 2023, roughly unchanged from the previous quarter (**Figure 2**). Outstanding Treasury and other government bonds and corporate bonds posted modest growth of 2.3% q-o-q and 0.4% q-o-q, respectively, due to subdued issuance during the quarter. Treasury and other government bonds outstanding (THB9.3 trillion) comprised over half of Thailand's LCY bond market at the end of September. Outstanding corporate bonds (THB4.8 trillion) and BOT bonds (THB2.4 trillion) represented the remaining 28.9% and 14.8%, respectively.

Figure 1: Thailand's Benchmark Yield Curve—
Local Currency Government Bonds

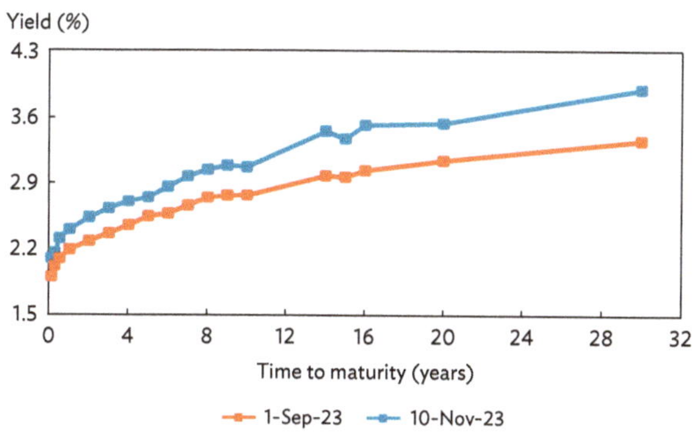

Sources: Based on data from Bloomberg LP and Thai Bond Market Association.

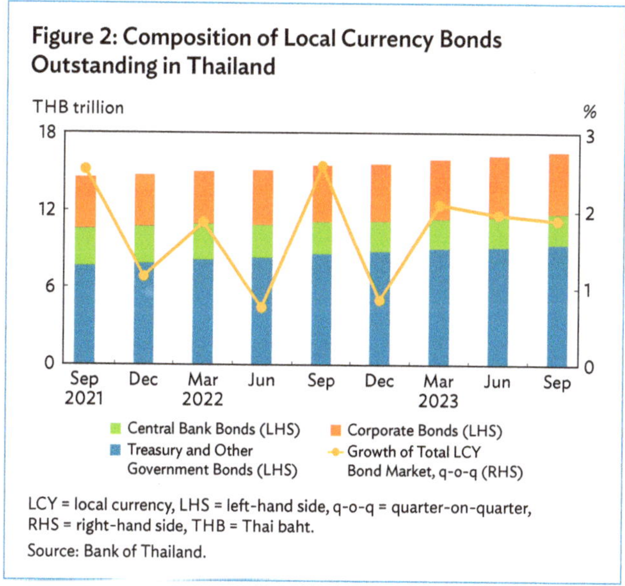

Figure 2: Composition of Local Currency Bonds
Outstanding in Thailand



LCY = local currency, LHS = left-hand side, q-o-q = quarter-on-quarter, RHS = right-hand side, THB = Thai baht.
Source: Bank of Thailand.

---

[12] Thai citizens aged 16 and above earning less than THB70,000 per month or with total bank deposits less than THB500,000 qualify for the cash handout.

**LCY bond issuance declined in Q3 2023 as bond sales contracted in both the public and corporate bond markets.** LCY bond issuance in Q3 2023 tallied THB2.2 trillion, down 10.0% from the second quarter of 2023 (**Figure 3**). Issuance of Treasury and other government bonds declined 15.4% q-o-q to THB535.8 billion as the government had previously frontloaded borrowing during preceding quarters. Meanwhile, corporate debt issuance totaled THB490.7 billion, down 19.9% q-o-q amid tighter BOT regulation of bond rollovers following an uptick in bond defaults. True Corporation was the largest issuer during the quarter with debt sales totaling THB29.1 billion.

## Investor Profile

**Domestic investors continued to hold a dominant share of Thai government bonds** (**Figure 4**). At the end of September, domestic investors' holdings accounted for nearly 90% of outstanding government bonds, up from 87.3% a year earlier. The sizable share of domestic investors contributes to Thai sovereign bonds' resilience to external shocks. During the same period, foreign investors' holdings of Thai government bonds declined slightly to 10.9% from 12.7%. Meanwhile, the BOT's holdings of government bonds increased from 5.3% to 6.6% from September 2022 to September 2023, as the central bank purchased a total of THB89.7 billion of government bonds to help stabilize the LCY bond market.

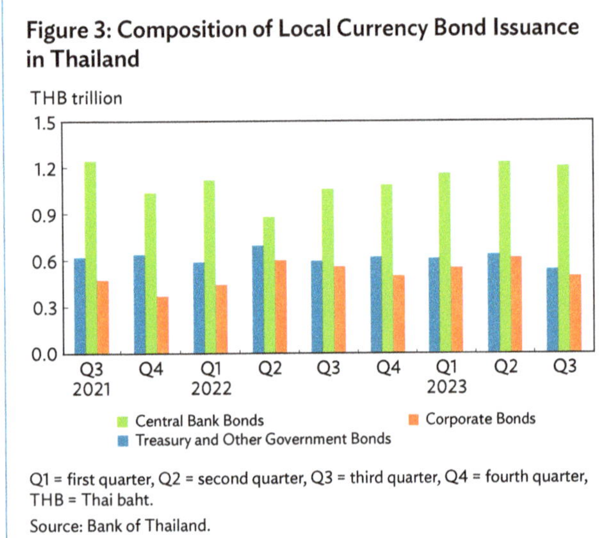

**Figure 3: Composition of Local Currency Bond Issuance in Thailand**



Q1 = first quarter, Q2 = second quarter, Q3 = third quarter, Q4 = fourth quarter, THB = Thai baht.
Source: Bank of Thailand.

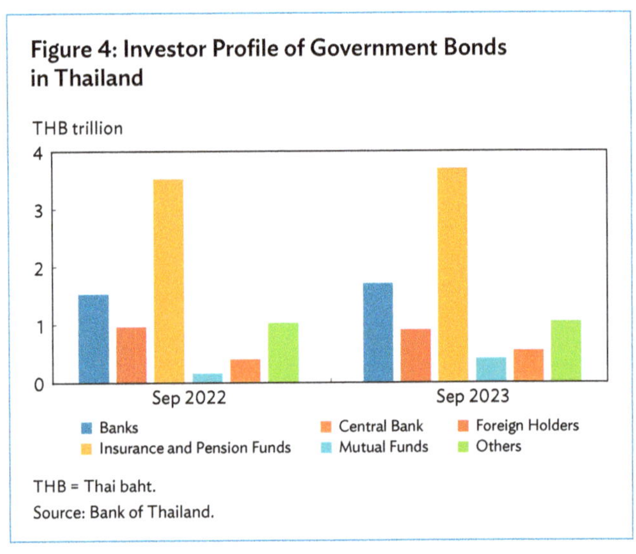

**Figure 4: Investor Profile of Government Bonds in Thailand**



THB = Thai baht.
Source: Bank of Thailand.

# Viet Nam

## Yield Movements

**Viet Nam's local currency (LCY) government bond yields climbed across all tenors between 1 September and 10 November due to an uptick in inflation and the United States Federal Reserve's decision to keep interest rates at a 22-year high in its September and November meetings (Figure 1).** Due to rising food and fuel prices, Viet Nam's year-on-year consumer price inflation, increased to 3.6% in October from 2.1% in July. However, it remained below the government's target of 4.5%.

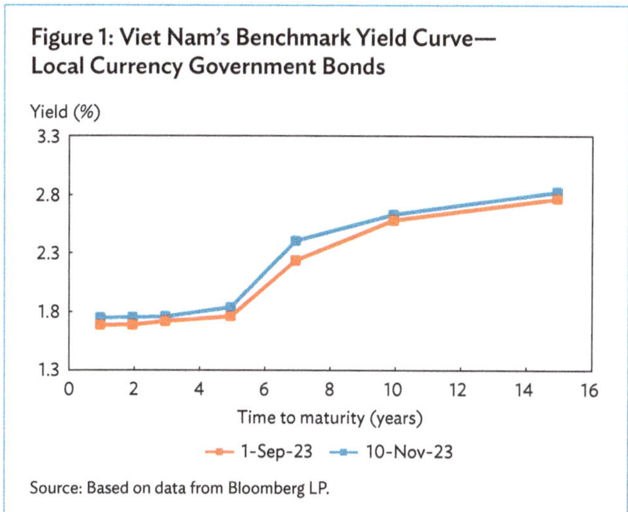

Figure 1: Viet Nam's Benchmark Yield Curve— Local Currency Government Bonds



Source: Based on data from Bloomberg LP.

## Local Currency Bond Market Size and Issuance

**The LCY bond market in Viet Nam grew 3.9% quarter-on-quarter (q-o-q) in the third quarter (Q3) of 2023, driven by the State Bank of Vietnam's (SBV) resumption of central bank securities issuance (Figure 2).** Amid slow credit growth, the SBV resumed issuance of central bank securities to mop up excess liquidity in the banking system. Growth in outstanding government bonds slowed to 1.5% q-o-q in Q3 2023 from the 3.3% q-o-q growth in the previous quarter due to the low volume of maturities and a decline in issuance. Meanwhile, corporate bonds contracted 3.1% q-o-q, driven by large volume of maturities in Q3 2023 despite strong corporate bond issuance. Per a news release from *The Investor*, Vietnamese broker VNDirect estimated that corporate bond maturities in August and September exceeded VND27.9 trillion and VND25.8 trillion, respectively, marking them among the largest monthly maturity values in 2023.

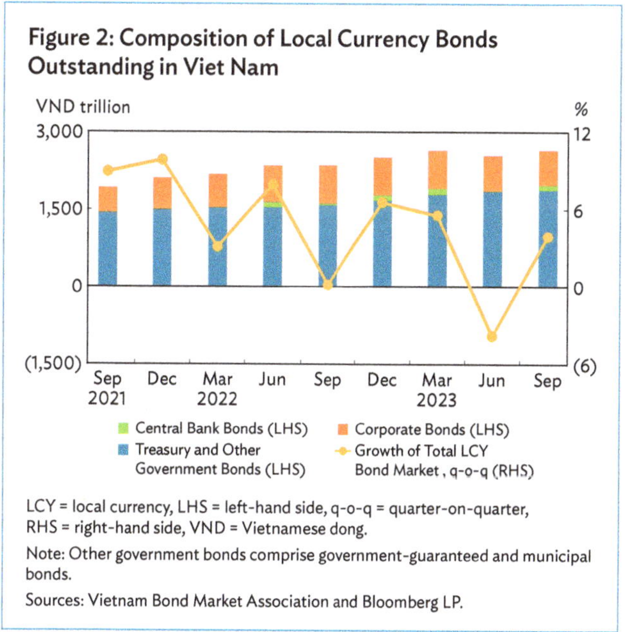

Figure 2: Composition of Local Currency Bonds Outstanding in Viet Nam



LCY = local currency, LHS = left-hand side, q-o-q = quarter-on-quarter, RHS = right-hand side, VND = Vietnamese dong.

Note: Other government bonds comprise government-guaranteed and municipal bonds.

Sources: Vietnam Bond Market Association and Bloomberg LP.

**Increased issuance from corporates drove total LCY bond issuance to expand 144.6% q-o-q to VND198.1 trillion in Q3 2023 (Figure 3).** Corporate bond issuance climbed more than threefold in Q3 2023 from the previous quarter as Vietnamese banks increased their issuance after the government issued circulars No. 2 and 3 in April, which removed some bottlenecks in debt payment rescheduling and bond repurchases. Bond issuance from the banking sector accounted for 59.0% of the economy's total LCY corporate bonds issued in Q3 2023, with the largest issuance coming from Asia Joint Stock Commercial Bank on aggregated debt sales of VND13.5 trillion. On the other hand, issuance of government bonds contracted 21.6% q-o-q as the government moderated issuance during the quarter, with some auctions not fully awarded. To help stabilize the foreign exchange market, the SBV resumed its issuance of central bank securities in September (VND93.8 trillion) since its last issuance in March 2023.

## Investor Profile

**At the end of September, insurance firms and banks continued to hold nearly all outstanding LCY government bonds in Viet Nam's market (Figure 4).** Collectively, their bond holdings accounted for 99.6% of the total, up from 99.4% in the same period a year earlier. Viet Nam had the highest Herfindahl–Hirschman Index score among its regional peers as the market has only two dominant investors.[13] Insurance companies remained the single-largest investor group with their holdings share declining to 59.7% at the end of September from 60.5% a year earlier, while the holdings share of banks increased to 39.9% from 38.9% in the same period. At the end of September 2023, securities companies and investment funds, nonresidents, and other investors held a marginal aggregate share of 0.4%.

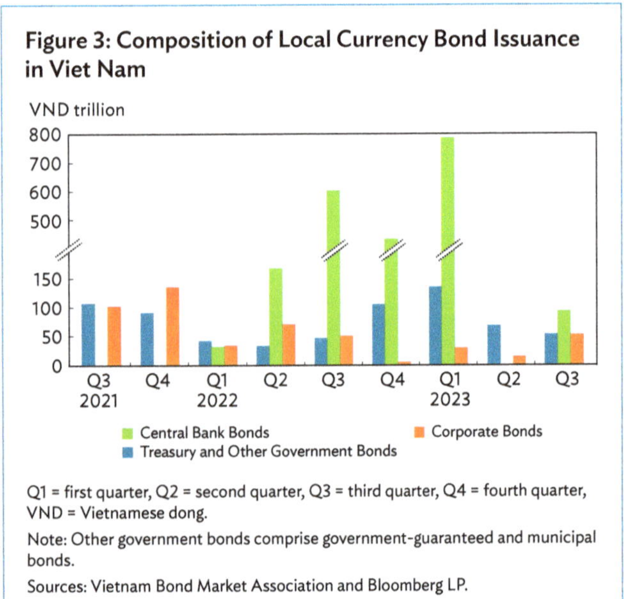

**Figure 3: Composition of Local Currency Bond Issuance in Viet Nam**



Q1 = first quarter, Q2 = second quarter, Q3 = third quarter, Q4 = fourth quarter, VND = Vietnamese dong.

Note: Other government bonds comprise government-guaranteed and municipal bonds.

Sources: Vietnam Bond Market Association and Bloomberg LP.

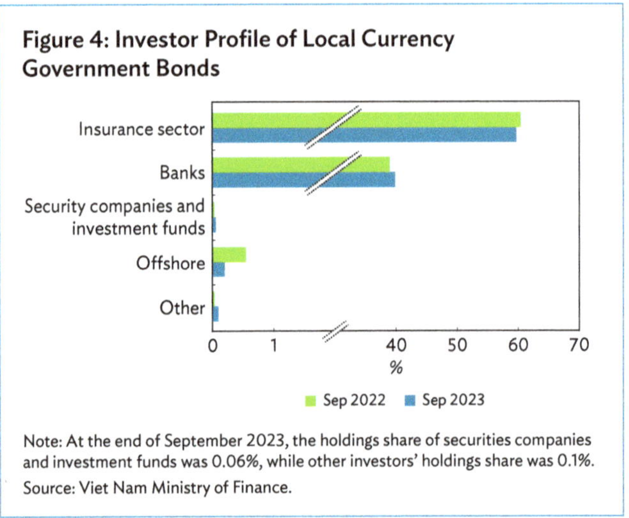

**Figure 4: Investor Profile of Local Currency Government Bonds**



Note: At the end of September 2023, the holdings share of securities companies and investment funds was 0.06%, while other investors' holdings share was 0.1%.

Source: Viet Nam Ministry of Finance.

---

[13] The Herfindahl–Hirschman Index is a commonly accepted measure of market concentration. In this case, the index is used to measure the investor profile diversification of the LCY bond market and is calculated by summing the squared share of each investor group in the bond market.